CIRAK

I0348237

THE FIVE LEVELS
OF
AWARENESS

A MANUAL FOR INNER PEACE AND OUTER PURPOSE

All rights reserved. No part of this book may be reproduced by any mechanical, photographic, or electronic process or in the form of a phonographic recording, nor may it be stored in a retrieval system, transmitted, or otherwise copied for public or private use without the publisher's prior written consent.

The author does not dispense medical advice or prescribe any technique as a form of treatment for physical, emotional, or medical problems without the advice of a physician, either directly or indirectly. The author's intent is only to offer information of a general nature to help you in your quest for emotional and spiritual well-being. Should you use any of the information in this book for yourself, the author and the publisher assume no responsibility for your actions.

Cirak and the tree ring logo are registered trademarks of Cirak Inc.

Editor: Michael Cirak
Photography: Dimas Surya Hariyanto
Coordinator: Yacinta Sri Nastiti Haryono
Iconography: Flaticon.com
Website: cirak.com

Copyright © 2025 Cirak 1st Edition ISBN: 978-1-7350140-4-3

"In all chaos there is a cosmos, in all disorder a secret order."

~ C.G. Jung

CONTENTS

LEVEL 1	5
LEVEL 1 | Lessons	7
LEVEL 1 | Reflections	29
LEVEL 1 | Paradoxes	33
LEVEL 1 | Summary	39
LEVEL 1 | Next Steps	43
LEVEL 2	49
LEVEL 2 | Lessons	51
LEVEL 2 | Reflections	75
LEVEL 2 | Paradoxes	81
LEVEL 2 | Summary	89
LEVEL 2 | Next Steps	91

LEVEL 3	95
LEVEL 3 | Lessons	97
LEVEL 3 | Reflections	123
LEVEL 3 | Paradoxes	133
LEVEL 3 | Summary	139
LEVEL 3 | Next Steps	143
LEVEL 4	147
LEVEL 4 | Lessons	149
LEVEL 4 | Reflections	173
LEVEL 4 | Paradoxes	181
LEVEL 4 | Summary	187
LEVEL 4 | Next Steps	191
LEVEL 5	199
LEVEL 5 | Lessons	201
LEVEL 5 | Reflections	219
LEVEL 5 | Paradoxes	233
LEVEL 5 | Summary	237
LEVEL 5 | Next Steps	243
TAKEAWAYS	247
EXAMPLES	285

CIRAK

THE FIVE LEVELS OF AWARENESS

A MANUAL FOR INNER PEACE AND OUTER PURPOSE

PREFACE

Ask anybody if their life has gone according to plan, and the response is usually ironic laughter, a roll of the eyes, and a telling look that it wasn't even close to what they envisioned. That's because anyone who's lived a few years has experienced the impossible-to-predict twists and turns your life can take. Even on the day-to-day level, the interplay of events, large and small, is so vast that even the most talented novelists or screenwriters struggle to recreate that sense of *you can't make this up*. Nothing is more creative than life happening because everything happens differently than you expect.

But if you ask those same people, if given the choice, would they choose a different life than the one they've lived? The answer is typically a resounding *no*. Why is that? You would think that when your life happens contrary to your expectations, you would rightfully be disappointed and wouldn't hesitate for a moment to give it all back. So why don't you?

It's because your wisdom is tied to your struggles. Once you come out on the other side, there is a deep-rooted sense that every failure is actually a success, every loss a gain, and every mundane moment a meaningful step in taking you down the road you're meant to travel to become the person you are today. Not a single step or misstep you've taken can be discounted. That's why, when given the choice, you cannot imagine wanting another life than the one you have lived. And if you're someone who's struggling at the moment and you *can* imagine giving some or all of it back, it only means you're in the middle of some core lessons, which is what this book is all about.

The Five Levels of Awareness outlines the evolution of your consciousness as it plays out in everyday life. Every person must pass through these levels on their journey through the physical dimension. Each level has its associated behaviors, attitudes, perspectives, and core lessons to help you graduate from one level to the next. As such, this book does not stipulate what you should do. Rather, it looks at what you are doing, what it says about you, and where the growth opportunities lie to move forward and live your best life possible.

As you read through these pages, resist the tendency to judge yourself if you find you're not at the desired level. Awareness is never about labeling yourself as right or wrong, better or worse, higher or lower. It's about accepting where you are and taking action to suffer less, thrive more, discover your true purpose, and fulfill your highest potential.

Lastly, should you ever feel triggered by what you read, recognize that feeling triggered is an invitation to greater self-awareness, which is the whole point of reading this book. Let feeling triggered illuminate insights into yourself and help you shift into a more authentic place. The more genuinely you self-reflect, the more personal growth you experience. By the end of this book, you will understand that life is a win-win situation.

So, what level of awareness are you?

LEVEL 1

"To"

Welcome to Level 1 awareness. The theme for this level is "To" because you think there is life, and there is you. And whenever anything happens, it happens *to* you.

You can already tell that at Level 1, there's a lot of friction in your life. You're constantly at odds with your environment. You think the world is out to get you, that resources are scarce, and that you must fight for your slice of the pie lest you wind up with nothing. You regret the past, resent the present, and are anxious about the future. You're afraid of wasting your life if you don't meet expectations.

But most of all, you reject yourself. You're unhappy with your body, your looks, your personality, your family. You keep blaming the people, places, and things around you for how you feel and insist that they behave so as not to trigger you. You think everyone else has it better, and everywhere you look, you find reasons why you deserve to be deeply unhappy with your lot in life.

You're so mired in combating yourself and the world around you that making time for personal development isn't even on your radar. All you do is get through the days, numb out when you can, hope that somehow something will change, and commiserate with others in the meantime.

Level 1 is the most emotionally demanding stage of your evolution because you don't see the connection between your lack of awareness and the chaos and dissatisfaction in your life. You just suffer and don't know why.

But don't worry. You're not alone. Everyone born into the physical dimension starts at Level 1 and must learn the same core lessons. No one gets special treatment, and no one is exempt. Even Jesus and the Buddha had to learn their lessons and undergo massive personal growth, as evident by their long, winding, and rather excruciating journeys.

Level 1 lessons reach deep into your psyche to surface stuck feelings and expose blind behavioral patterns. Even after mastering them, more refinement is needed in later stages. Following are the main Level 1 lessons:

LEVEL 1 | Lessons

Lesson 1
VICTIMHOOD

When you first enter the physical dimension and in the first years of growing up, there is a sense of limitlessness, of *anything goes*. You get the impression that you're the captain of your ship, the master of your fortunes. It feels like the world is your unrestricted playground, and you get to make up the rules.

Quickly, however, you realize this is not the case. You're not actually in control. Life keeps happening differently than you expect. It keeps unfolding in ways you cannot prevent or predict. You're always playing catch-up to your happiness. Whenever you achieve any success, it fades before you can truly enjoy it. You keep waiting for something to happen, that feeling of having arrived and for your life to begin. But the years roll by, and that feeling never comes.

Life starts out so promising. You think you can have your cake and eat it, too. But before you know it, you find yourself fighting for scraps. Nothing of the life you've envisioned for yourself is coming together. Increasingly, your earthly experience looks like one big disappointment. It feels like you've been lied to on the grandest scale.

No doubt, living with Level 1 awareness is a rough existence. Everything really does feel like it's happening *to* you. You might even describe your relationship with life as abusive. The world keeps beating up on you and your plans. You should be forgiven if you feel like a victim.

Of course, the world is not out to get you. You're just abusing yourself with your thoughts about the world. But you don't realize that yet. You're primarily driven to act out your conditioning. You keep complaining and blaming because everyone around you is doing the same. It's almost like you're waiting for something to happen so you can gossip about what others did to you, never realizing you're just reinforcing your sense of victimhood. In this environment, finding fault in everyone but yourself is entirely normal.

In fact, you're so identified with being a victim that you think adversity is only happening to you. You're entirely convinced that your misery is uniquely yours, that everyone else has it much easier, and that life is being extra unfair to you.

But life is not unfair. You just haven't taken ownership of your thoughts and feelings. Nor have you realized that most of the things you feel triggered by aren't even yours. It's baggage you've inherited from your circumstances growing up. In your formative years, your brain is like a sponge without filters. You absorb everything parents, teachers, peers, society, and the media say, internalizing it as *this is me*. You wind up carrying whatever ideas of fear, scarcity, and lack you're bombarded with into adulthood, and then you wake up one day wondering how life got so complicated.

But everything has its purpose. From this Level 1 chaos, the first seeds of awareness are sown. You feel like there must be a better way to live your life. At first, you think that finding a better way means trying harder. You think it means planning better and controlling more. The Level 1 mind is entirely unprepared to surrender its beliefs. You cannot imagine letting go of the vision of the life you want, the vision you feel you were promised early on. So you keep arguing and fighting with life, even though you're not making any headway. This can go on for quite a while. But gradually, as life beats you up, you soften up.

Granted, the last thing you want to hear is that getting beat up by life is good for you. But suffering drives you forward.

By experiencing what you don't want, you learn what you do want. Level 1 is all about contrast, shaping you into the person you're meant to be by making you dig deeper than you're comfortable with, bringing out your innermost qualities. Nothing does this better than feeling like a victim.

At this stage, it may not be readily apparent why personal growth depends on accepting circumstances you don't like. But all your frustration from not getting the life you want is preparing you to live your best life ever.

Lesson 2
SEPARATENESS

Underlying your victim mentality is a deep identification with separateness. There is you, and there is the tree. There is you, and there is your dog. There is you, and there is your partner, your children, your house, your car, the moon. There is you, and there is everything else. Everything is its own thing. At Level 1, you think you're a separate entity among a multitude of other separate entities.

There is a simple and obvious reason for this sense of separateness: your mind.

The story of Adam and Eve perfectly depicts how this separateness came to be. Initially, the two are part of unity consciousness, enjoying the infinite peace and abundance that flows from being one with the source of all creation. But then they eat from the Tree of Knowledge and get pulled into their heads. They start believing their thoughts and begin judging things, and a divide emerges between themselves and the world around them. This shift from a pure state of being to living in mind-made separateness represents their expulsion from paradise.

The same thing has happened to you. You've been conditioned to live in your head, obsessed with labeling, defining, and analyzing everything you encounter. You're not wrong to want to explore the physical dimension—it's an incredible place! But trying to judge your way through life makes you lonely, afraid, and miserable. You cut yourself off from loving your life.

The suffering from feeling separate is substantial. You lack trust or confidence in life. You're anxious that the odds are stacked against you. Because when you think it's you against the Universe, they are. You're constantly overwhelmed and unsure of what step to take next. The world keeps reinforcing that you should be better at planning and judging, but all that does is separate you even more from the world. You look around and see everybody else doing the same. Everyone lives in their little separate madhouse. But nobody notices it because everyone's copying each other.

The primary Level 1 task is to judge less and allow more. Blame less and accept more. Think less and feel more. Hate less and love more. It's a long, drawn-out process that impacts all areas of your life. But this is how you gradually come out of separateness and back together to have a shared and mutually respectful experience of your common humanity. You might be thinking, *Why does life have to be so complicated? Why can't I just be happy?* Well, you can. But that's exactly what gets in the way of it: *thinking.*

Lesson 3
ABSENT-MINDEDNESS

Being absent-minded means your body is here, but your mind is elsewhere. You're thinking about things that have nothing to do with what's currently happening. The most amazing sunset, the ideal love interest, or the business opportunity of a lifetime could be right in front of you. Yet, you miss it because you're lost in thought.

While you're lost in thought, you're not just absent-minded. You're lost to your senses. The sights, sounds, and smells of your environment become muted. It takes a loud, sharp knock or sound to snap you out of this state. Being lost in thought is also when you're most likely to get into an accident. Accidents happen when you're not paying attention. And not just physical accidents. When you're absent-minded, you also make bad decisions.

Absent-mindedness begins with believing your thoughts. Whenever a thought comes along, you accept its content as something you must engage with. You haven't yet developed the ability to choose which thoughts to give your attention to. Each new thought takes you over completely, pulling you down the rabbit hole of overthinking.

There, you keep replaying certain situations, accompanied by an ongoing mental commentary of how you should have said this or that or what you will do next time it happens. The Level 1 mind doesn't grasp that you can't change an incident once it's happened. Nor can you prepare for the future because nothing happens the same way twice. Even if the elements of a situation were exactly the same, reality always feels different than your projections about it.

Absent-mindedness is the single biggest drain on your life. It's the state that gives rise to anxiety and fear. The noise in your head becomes overwhelming, and your creativity comes to a grinding halt. You stress about all the things that *could* or *should* happen. You're constantly ruminating about *what if.* Then you get burnt out or bored and think there's something wrong with you. You put so much time and effort into living a long and healthy life. Yet, you're not present most of the time because you're thinking about things that make you sick.

There is substantial research on mind-wandering, what Western psychology calls *rumination.* The typical person spends half their day lost in thought. With Level 1 awareness, you can expect this to be even higher. It's no wonder then that you're exhausted. It's no wonder you feel lost. You don't know yourself outside of this constant entanglement with thoughts. You think your value to society is based on how well you can think. Then, you try to find yourself somewhere in all that thinking activity. You think you are who you think you are.

The solution to staying out of the trap of overthinking is to become more aware of your thoughts. Then, you are free to engage only with thoughts that benefit you. But this is not so easy. You are deeply attached to your thoughts. You've spent your whole life listening to and following your hyperactive mind. It has you convinced that your thoughts are real, solid, and reliable and that thinking more is how you solve problems and get through life.

Yet, it's easy to see how the opposite is the case. Most thoughts are simply not true because they're either replaying the past or trying to predict the future, both of which are pure fabrications of the mind. Furthermore, if you probe deeper, you quickly find that thoughts are incredibly fickle, flippant, and unstable. It's called *the monkey mind* for a reason. It can't stay focused on anything for more than a few seconds.

Try it out for yourself. Focus on the breath at the entrance of your nostrils. There's a sensitive area there, below the nostrils and above the upper lip, where you can feel the touch of your incoming and outgoing breath. If you have trouble locating your breath, you can breathe slightly harder once or twice, and once you feel your breath, return to natural breathing. Go ahead and put all your attention on that sensitive spot. Do it for one minute, and then continue reading.

How long did it take before thoughts about other things pulled your attention away? Unless you're an experienced meditator, you likely can't keep your attention on your breath for more than a few seconds.

This inability to stay focused on something as basic as your breath can be shocking at first. Realizing that your mind is about as steady as a flickering candle is not exactly reassuring.

But that's what you've been working with all your life. This mind that can't stay still. It can't let anything just be. It constantly looks to control, define, and predict the next unknown moment. It obsessively labels things as good or bad, right or wrong, pleasant or unpleasant, to make it known and then moves on. One could say this is a holdover from an earlier point in evolution when the mind needed to protect you from imminent danger. But in the modern world, this behavior is misplaced. The result is constant mental chatter that keeps you feeling separate, lost, and confused.

Another way to discern how erratic your thoughts are is by questioning them. Often, you can dissolve thoughts that have long tormented you simply by asking yourself *is this true?* This works because you must be aware of the thought in order to ask the question. And that means you're no longer identified with the thought. The basic principle is when you experience things from awareness, they have no power over you. Questioning your thoughts is like poking a hole in the balloons of your beliefs and watching them pop.

Another exercise to break up old thought patterns is to keep your attention on your pinky finger for a minute. Examine it intently, looking at the tiniest details, all its creases and folds. After a while, it will start looking odd and foreign, as if you've never seen this peculiar appendage before. If you stay with it long enough, this sentiment spreads to other fingers, your hand, arm, and the rest of your body. It can suddenly feel surreal that you even exist—that anything exists. That's because when you're extremely focused on the details of something, thoughts about it fade away, and you're just in your pure experience of it. You move past your mental labels and definitions and into a nebulous space where you realize nothing is anything. Doing that gets increasingly uncomfortable because you are dissolving the reality upon which you've built your identity and view of the world, which otherwise is held together by nothing but a thin layer of beliefs that needs constant reinforcement. And if you stop reinforcing them, that reality ceases to exist – including yourself.

Another classic characteristic of thoughts is that they're repetitive. The vast majority of thoughts you think daily are the same thoughts you thought yesterday, the day before, and the day before that. In fact, you very rarely think of anything new because the mind only knows what it already knows. What keeps you up at night is not a breath-taking smattering of novel ideas and ground-breaking concepts. What keeps you up at night is a handful of endlessly repetitive thought loops that take you down the same rabbit holes as the night before. And even though it drives you nuts, you might say this endless repetition is by design, as it reinforces existing beliefs, which your mind loves. Because if you stop believing, your whole mind-made reality threatens to fall apart.

Also, most of your thoughts are negative. Again, this could be a holdover from the past when humans needed to be more alert to immediate dangers in their environment. Fortunately, there are few imminent threats today, but the mind is still wired to look for them. It looks to fulfill its purpose of protecting you by amplifying insignificant issues. Think of office politics or family dynamics as prominent examples where a nothing burger routinely leads to major drama.

An alternative explanation of why you're wired for negativity is a more insidious one. The mind is an absolute control freak. It could very well be spewing those negative thoughts in order to keep you in fear and it firmly in the driver's seat. After all, there's no better vehicle for staying in control than fear. From that perspective, it seems reasonable to think the mind favors negative thoughts because they ensure you stay identified with your mind.

Much has been written about positive psychology. But even if you could only think positively, it wouldn't make a difference. The main issue with your mind is not its inherent negativity. The main issue is that you can't switch it off. It's always on. It won't leave you alone, even when you desperately want it to, so you can get some rest.

Your busy mind keeps you up at night and occupies you during the day, adversely affecting everything you do. You don't sleep well, eat well, or listen well. You're not able to focus or enjoy yourself. No matter how expensive your front-row seats are at the theater, you can't stay present enough to appreciate the show. Choice overload and analysis paralysis make even simple tasks like shopping torture. You stay mired in constant comparison and self-judgment. All you see is lack and scarcity. You are ruled by fear and limiting beliefs. Your productivity and outlook on life suffer. There are many challenges in life. But the noise in your head is the biggest one.

Living in your head consumes your resources, depletes your energy, and limits your perspective to self-preservation. It prevents you from seeing yourself as an expression of the life force that inhabits everything, including the trillions of cells working in unison to create you. The Level 1 mind is utterly blind to the sheer miracle of your existence.

Lesson 4
ATTACHMENTS

Level 1 teaches you how to discern between healthy and unhealthy attachments. Greater awareness of the differences can have an immediate positive impact on your quality of life.

Attachments are energetic connections that form between people, animals, places, and things. More specifically, you become attached to the feeling those things evoke in you. You can become attached to your dog, house, car, money, or memories as much as a life partner.

At first, this doesn't seem like a problem. And it isn't. Forming attachments is normal and inevitable. Whenever you engage with anyone or anything, an energetic exchange happens and a connection is invoked, even if only in the slightest, seemingly unnoticed way. You can think of it as *touching each others lives.* Forming attachments to your environment is the essential experience of life in the physical plane.

However, attachments become unhealthy when they contain conditions, expectations, or dependencies. With these behaviors, you make others responsible for filling the void of what you're missing inside, putting tremendous pressure on the relationship. Any shift in the dynamic causes friction. Whatever the conditions are covering up - such as a lack of self-worth or fear of abandonment - is exposed. Even small changes in schedule or routines, or when someone sets new boundaries, can cause disruption and upset in the elaborate control grid a Level 1 traveler creates to avoid looking at themselves.

In fact, at Level 1, most of your attachments are unhealthy. Most of the connections you have formed to the world around you contain some element of clinging, craving, resisting, and controlling. At this point in your evolution, you still think manipulating your environment is what life is about. That demanding certain behaviors from others means you care for them. That wanting to dominate is a virtue. You're not yet aware that this is all compensation and avoidance behavior.

One of the most unhealthy attachments of the Level 1 mind is to outside influences. Here, you care deeply about how you are perceived, affecting your confidence and peace of mind. Opinions backed by many people carry even more leverage, impacting what direction you take in life. It's easy to lose yourself in outside voices that appear to quell your inner anxiety. You find yourself gravitating towards crowds, mimicking social behavior, going around virtue signaling, glued to the latest news and trends, unable to recognize that everything you hear, read, and see is just someone else's view of the world and is motivated by *their* truth, not yours.

By joining the crowd, you get pulled into the feeling of being part of something bigger than just dealing with your personal issues. Surrendering your troubled identity to that of the collective is like throwing a giant blanket over all your wounds and worries about not being good enough. It creates a layer of noise that distracts you from your fears of loneliness and anxiety about your future. The group dynamic supersedes the self and gives you the impression that your life is under control and has meaning.

But don't worry. You cannot avoid your evolution. Experiencing groupthink is one of the most important lessons. The longer you are lost to yourself, the more contrast builds to your true self. The sense that you're not living your own life reaches a tipping point that catapults you out of the group and onto your path of self-realization.

Lastly, as a Level 1 traveler, you're also particularly attached to your physical form. How could you not be? You've just arrived in your body, injected into a world of senses and sensations. An endless multiplicity of sights, sounds, scents, tastes, and touches beckons you to join the celebration of aliveness. The physical world is constantly reaching out to you, wanting to pull you into the infinite detail, quietly calling attention to the impossibility of its existence and the incredible intelligence behind it. You should not feel guilty for being seduced into everything the physical dimension has to offer.

Indeed, the material world won't let you go so easily. In fact, your attachments to the physical are like superglue. Look how you keep insisting life should happen your way. Look how you keep planning and getting upset when things happen differently. Look how you can't stop thinking and keep reacting to your thoughts and feelings. Look how you cling to what you believe is true and resist change at all costs. This way of living is cemented in you like the foundation of a skyscraper.

No wonder it takes forever for new insights to form about the nature of your existence. No wonder it takes deep trauma for you to let go of the control you think you have. This trauma, in turn, takes forever to heal from, affecting you and everyone in your environment, often for generations. With Level 1 life skills and emotional intelligence, the process is gradual and tedious, and progress is barely noticeable. It only makes rational sense for reincarnation to exist. You couldn't possibly master all Level 1 lessons in one lifetime, let alone those at higher levels of awareness yet to come.

Letting go of unhealthy attachments can be more challenging than it seems because it is coupled with a massive fear of change. Even when you know a particular situation is unhealthy - perhaps a dead-end job or toxic relationship - it can still be hard to get out of it, so great is the fear of the unknown. As the saying goes, *the devil you know is better than the one you don't.* That's why implementing change is a gradual process. Your suffering needs to outweigh your fear of the unknown before you invite corrective measures.

Looking closely, you can see how fear of the unknown is an unhealthy attachment to your imagination. You're not afraid of what is happening. You're afraid of what you imagine *might* happen. You feel compelled to control what could happen if you don't. For the Level 1 mind, one of the hardest things to accept is that your plan—and all the hopes and dreams you've attached to it—might not be the plan life has in store for you. To let go of whatever milestones you've set for yourself - be it in your career, lifestyle, or relationships - means letting go of the controlled vision of the future you've constructed in your head. Deconstructing this future does not happen without significant yelling, kicking, and screaming.

Lesson 5
KNOWLEDGE

The Level 1 mind thinks it can know life. It thinks it can organize everything into neat compartments of right and wrong, good and bad, real and unreal, and call it *truth*. It loves to latch onto narratives inherited from your lineage, promoted by education, approved by science, reinforced by history, hammered in by politics, and upheld by what the collective consensus calls *facts*. Any message claiming to know how life works is a soothing balm for the mind on its singular mission of planning out your life ahead of living it.

What makes knowledge so appealing is that it gives you confidence in a permanent and predictable world. But this is one grand illusion. Every definition contains countless fleeting elements, including the context of who you are, where you are, who you're with, confirmation bias, sanctioned perspectives of your profession, who commissioned the research, generational and cultural factors, etc. Even your mood, time of day, and whether you're hungry or tired influence how you interpret data. Thus, every so-called fact is contextual, and no context ever repeats. Every finding is unique and becomes outdated the moment you formulate it.

As such, there's never a moment where you can truly know something. Nothing is knowable because everything is always in motion. Everything keeps changing and evolving. Even if you had all the memory, storage, and processing power in the world, life never stands still long enough for you to be able to say something *is* something. Nothing is something for more than the blink of a moment.

Once you think you know something, it loses its aliveness. It's no longer happening—it's already part of the past. Your knowing of it creates separateness again, keeping you stuck in your mind's definitions and labels, essentially surrounded by dead things. If this is what you build your life around, it's no wonder you feel disconnected and lonely and that life is happening *to* you.

Curiously, the mind is not concerned with the consequences of feeling separate, even if it leads to anxiety, depression, and fear. Instead, it is singularly focused on knowing things because knowing something makes it seem fixed and predictable. From there, it can be factored into your plans for predicting the future. And thus, the illusion grows that the

LEVEL 1 | LESSONS

more you know, the easier life gets and the more successful you will be.

But it's not just living in an illusion. That which you celebrate as knowledge comes at a tremendous cost. Not only are you left with the great fallacy that you know something, but you're imprinted with the picture of a static world into which you can project your goals and reasonably expect to achieve them. This is what leads you to feel like a victim in the first place. You become entirely cordoned off from considering that many other forces are at play than just your wants and needs. This is why you feel so lonely in a big, scary world.

It's ironic that your greatest obstacle to growing your awareness is what you value the most: your knowledge. But don't worry. Level 1 will continue to show you the fallibility of planning your life based on what you think you know. This lesson might not come easily, but it's sure to come.

Finally, it's important to note that the mind should not be vilified. To truly honor the temporary structure of whatever you're experiencing would require the mind to formulate a constant sequence of new definitions, one for each new impression. It would be impractical and overwhelming to operate this way. It's much more feasible to slap a broad label on it.

That aside, the mind is a fantastic instrument that can receive and translate external stimuli into physical sensations, provide context and situational awareness, and synthesize complex information into digestible chunks. It also makes your heart beat, regulates your body's autonomous functions, and stores your experience in memory so you don't have to learn the same tasks over and over again. It's an amazing tool if you use it for its intended purpose.

It's also great for gathering information and executing once you've made a decision. But the decision itself cannot come from the mind. It cannot come from feeling separate. It cannot come from your mental labels of things. It can only come from your inner truth.

LEVEL 1 | Reflections

Level 1 is a tough place because you're unaware of your limiting beliefs and self-harming behaviors. The silver lining is that some refuge can be found in ignorance. Still, the lessons hit you hard and fast, like a boxer fighting a ghost, not knowing where the blows are coming from, far from realizing it's your own mind.

COMPARISON

The mind loves to compare itself to others, usually looking for validation of its knowledge. But all this constant comparison does is fuel your inner critic. You're always looking around to prove to yourself that others have it easier. Oh, how strong that victim mindset is.

Assume for a moment that whoever you're comparing yourself to does, indeed, have it easier. Maybe they've done the inner work to be where they are now. Maybe they've already been through the darkness and have come out on the other side. You can't look at somebody's profile and know the trials and tribulations they've been through. You can't tell by how they're dressed if their life resembles anything close to how they wanted it to go.

You just can't know the twists and turns a person's life has taken. Those who seem to have it easier may be coming off the tail end of many lifetimes full of struggle. And unless you've experienced regression therapy, you can't know the twists and turns your own life has taken, either.

Ultimately, blame, jealousy, and thinking others have it better are nothing but self-harm. Comparing yourself to others never leads to a more positive outlook. Moving through Level 1 means learning to focus on yourself, knowing that everyone has to jump through the same hoops, and now it's your turn. Whatever others do is no longer your concern. You can trust that no one gets a free ride. You're just meeting them at their current station in life. At one point, they were just like you. At one point, you will be just like them. The only sure thing is that everyone has to master the same five levels of awareness.

CONTRAST

Many people see the spiritual path but aren't quite ready to dedicate themselves to it. They know there is a deeper essence to themselves but don't feel called to go there yet. No problem. Live out your attachments and habit patterns fully. They contain more lessons to be learned. Remember, all your actions build contrast—between the expectations you create and the life that actually happens. This contrast pushes you forward. It's not a bad thing. It's simply what is needed for the energies to play themselves out so you can move forward. Contrast is superfood for your journey. The tension from trying to control the uncontrollable, predict the unpredictable, and feeling separate eventually catapults you to higher levels of awareness.

SUFFERING

While Level 1 is full of suffering, the good news is that life won't let you suffer forever. This is somewhat cynical, given that life has empowered you to create your own suffering in the first place. But alas, there's no use complaining or questioning the wisdom of the Universe.

What matters is that you would rather sit here reading this book than be out frolicking with the crowd. That you would rather heal inner wounds and reach higher consciousness than indulge in mind-numbing escapism speaks volumes. That facing emotional pain is more important than avoiding it points to a deep commitment to self-love. No longer being afraid to feel your feelings shows your readiness to go deeper and discover life's inner workings. You are taking your well-being into your own hands, dissolving blockages, and graduating to higher realms of awareness.

LEVEL 1 | Paradoxes

Paradoxes are what make your healing journey so challenging. How the mind assumes things work is often exactly opposite to how they actually do. But that's only because you've been conditioned by a Level 1 world ruled by the five senses, where anything you can't see, taste, touch, smell, or feel isn't considered real. It disavows even the most basic principles of how the Universe works, which is based on energy.

All paradoxes share the same characteristic: they point to the path of least resistance. For a paradox to sink in, you must be open to the unknown and show a genuine interest to let a deeper truth reveal itself. When it does, it's like lightning strikes. A whole new world opens up, and a piece of life's puzzle clicks into place.

Taking time to unravel paradoxes is an effective way to expand your awareness and worldview. They make you realize that you've been working much harder than you need to. That life is designed to be easy and uncomplicated. That you're going against universal principles when something is difficult. You also wake up to how remarkable it is that you can be oriented one particular way, swearing it is the truth. And then, in an instant, grasping a paradox dissolves a big piece of your truth structure, and you see the world with completely new eyes.

Here are the most common paradoxes you encounter at Level 1:

PARADOX #1

Pushing away feelings keeps them stuck.

This is an obvious one that everyone can relate to. Yet, it's one of the hardest realizations to internalize.

You become conditioned to push away feelings you don't like feeling. But that's how they stay stuck. Anything you resist, an energetic chord forms that binds you to it. By pushing away uncomfortable emotions, they get buried. But they're still there. When something in your environment triggers you, stuck feelings come roaring back to the surface, often much more intense than before.

That's because each time you push down a feeling, you add more energy to the ball of unresolved emotions. It grows and hits you harder each time it surfaces. If you refuse to confront it and keep pushing it back down, some of the pressurized energy seeps into other parts of your body, becoming a physical malady. If this goes on long enough, it becomes so severe it can kill you.

Once again, the solution is to learn to let things be as they are. Feelings are no different. It may be hard at first to break the patterns of reactivity. But once you get the hang of it, it's life-changing. You realize all feelings come and go, no matter how difficult they are. You recognize that being at the mercy of your environment dictating how you feel is no way to live. To be truly free, your feelings must be free to arise and pass.

PARADOX #2

The answer comes when you stop thinking about it.

Thinking isn't just an aspect of the mind. It's its sole purpose. All it does is think, think, think. Think your way to every answer. Think your way out of every dilemma. Think about the past and the future. Re-think things you've already thought of. Think about what to think of next. This includes problems that don't exist yet but that you can imagine. In fact, anything you don't know yet is a problem because not knowing itself is a threat. Your entire future being unknown is the biggest concern of all.

There must be a better way to use the mind for what it's designed for. And there is. How often have you felt weary trying to remember something, so you let it go and turn your attention elsewhere, and suddenly, out of nowhere, the answer pops into your head?

This is your inner wisdom at work. The brain is great for absorbing information but cannot decide what option is right for you. That means the best use of your faculties is to define the problem, step away, and let the answer reveal itself. In fact, the more precisely you formulate the question, the closer to the answer you get. A perfectly structured question and its answer are almost identical.

PARADOX #3

The more you detach the closer you become.

Ironically, the Level 1 mind creates unhealthy attachments, thinking they will bring you closer to whomever you are attached to. But they actually keep you apart. An unhealthy attachment is when you expect someone else to fulfill something you're missing inside. That leads to a dynamic of dependency, including keeping you energetically and emotionally distant and unavailable.

Once you detach, however, the energetic dependency that holds you apart dissolves. And this is where something magical happens. One would expect detachment to result in both energies drifting apart. But the opposite happens. You gravitate towards one another. With the unhealthy part of your attachment gone, only the healthy part remains. And that brings you closer. What a beautiful design.

PARADOX #4

Your life happens when you stop trying to make it happen

No matter what your mind tells you or what the world around you tries to impress upon you, life cannot be predicted, planned, or controlled. Things never go according to plan. There are always unforeseens because you cannot foresee the future. There are always unknowns because you cannot know everything. All you can do is show up and respond to what's already there.

As long as you believe your thoughts, you stay small. As long as you insist on your plan, you suffer. But once you accept that you know nothing, your life can take on the direction and momentum it always wanted to, but that you were obstructing, thinking you knew better.

You don't have to make life happen before living it. Let living it shape you, form you, and take you on the wildest ride imaginable. Along the way, watch yourself turn into the confident, authentic, and complete person you always wanted to be.

LEVEL 1 | Summary

Level 1 is packed with fundamental lessons. These lessons help you diffuse self-imposed pressure and broaden your perspective so that you no longer feel like life is happening *to* you.

To master Level 1, you must work through feelings of victimhood and separateness, which dominate your life experience and account for much of your suffering. By establishing a mindfulness practice, you become more aware of your thoughts and spend less time absent-minded. This rewires your brain to react less, leading to clear decisions, healthy attachments, and shifting from relying on knowledge to navigating from your inner voice.

In summary, here are the main skills and behaviors you develop during Level 1. You can check off which ones you've mastered and build greater awareness around the ones that still need work. You're ready to graduate from Level 1 when:

☐ You understand that as long as you feel like a victim, you stay stuck in negativity.

☐ You realize how incredibly fickle and random your monkey mind is.

☐ You're shocked to realize how much time you spend lost in thought.

☐ You comprehend that pushing away your feelings keeps them stuck.

☐ You're aware that you're afraid of being alone.

☐ You understand that judging others makes you feel separate from them.

☐ You realize you keep insisting life should happen your way and that you get upset when it doesn't.

☐ You notice how often you get into arguments because you think you're right and everyone else is wrong.

☐ You realize you've been chasing outcomes because you believe your happiness depends on them.

☐ You notice you're afraid of change and how you try to create permanence in your life.

☐ You realize you're addicted to big emotions, big experiences. Feeling ecstatic is meaningful for you.

☐ You understand the difference between healthy and unhealthy attachments.

☐ You recognize how overrated and unreliable knowledge is.

- ☐ You notice how much time you spend thinking about how you come across to others.

- ☐ You can tell how constant comparison only leads to feeling bad about yourself.

- ☐ You understand that contrast gives you perspective.

- ☐ You sense there must be a better way and are ready to do something about your suffering.

LEVEL 1 | Next Steps

Don't worry if you can't check off all the boxes. At first, the depth and complexity of Level 1 awareness building might be overwhelming. You might question if you have what it takes to get through it. After all, you've spent your whole life reacting, resisting, and wanting things your way. You've spent decades over-anticipating, overthinking, and over-planning. Now, you find yourself hard-wired with certain behaviors and perspectives. Where does one begin to come out of it? And can the process be accelerated?

To graduate from Level 1, you must reverse the process: come out of your head and back into your body. Establishing a meditation practice is a must. Self-reflection through journaling or books like this should be ongoing. Movement exercises like nature walks, yoga, qi gong, and pilates must become part of your upgraded lifestyle. Pockets of stillness need to be established. Basic principles of well-being must be implemented, including better sleep, nutrition, exercise, and mental health. And an overall reduction of unnecessary stress is required. You cannot function properly if you're always in fight or flight mode. These elements provide the foundation and the fuel for doing the inner work.

Here are some straightforward steps to guide you through Level 1:

1. Spend mornings in Noble Silence. That means refraining from speaking for as long as possible until your first interaction, work call, or similar. If you absolutely must speak, do so softly and with clear intention, and then return to silence. Examine how silence makes you feel. Notice any discomfort and the tendency to cover it up with unnecessary chatter, checking messages, etc. Make the most of your mornings by extending the calmness you inherited from the previous night's sleep as far into the new day as possible.

2. Establish a morning self-care routine. This could involve a simple grounding activity like a taking a short walk, standing barefoot in the grass, or making yourself laugh by thinking of something funny. It can mean making a healthy breakfast and enjoying your morning coffee or tea with greater intention. It can involve tuning into how you feel today and picking out a matching wardrobe. It can also mean indulging in skincare and essential oils, playing calming music, or reading a chapter from your favorite book. If you're more adventurous, consider taking ice-cold showers. It shocks your circadian rhythm into starting the 24-hour cycle, making sure you get tired in the evening when you're supposed to sleep. It also leads to more psychological resilience because you regularly do something uncomfortable. And it trains your cold response so you stay healthy more easily during cold seasons. Whatever activity you choose, stay connected to your senses. Your senses connect you to your body and keep you engaged. That means feeling the fabric when making your bed or folding laundry. Take in the aroma and watch the swirls as you pour that cup of coffee. Feel the water, soap, and steam while taking that warm shower. Turn your existing daily routines into deeper sensory experiences. It's a fun, effective, and enriching way to become more embodied and sets the tone for the rest of your day. Most importantly, hold off looking at your phone, email, or messages until after your morning self-care routine.

3. Do breathwork. Do this simple breath exercise before you go into an important meeting, jump on a call, or sit down to respond to emails: Focus on the incoming and outgoing breath at the entrance of your nostrils. Look for the touch of your breath, and once you feel it, continue breathing naturally. Whenever you notice that your mind has drifted, simply notice it, and without frustration, bring your attention back to the touch of your breath at the entrance of your nostrils. Do this for at least 5 minutes a day. Even one in-and-out breath is effective in keeping you out of your head and in your body. This will be your go-to meditation as you move into higher levels of awareness.

4. Start a daily journaling practice. Journaling is a powerful processing tool. While thoughts are floating around in your head, they're incredibly vague and erratic. Writing them down forces you to use more scrutiny and apply boundaries. Often, this results in the realization that the thought isn't true or is way overblown. Put down at least three sentences, even if you don't know what to write about. See if more flows from there. Journaling once or twice daily can significantly help process emotions and relieve the pressure from overthinking.

5. Get comfortable not knowing. The next time a question arises that you don't know the answer to, resist the urge to look it up. Notice what it feels like in your body not to know something and practice getting comfortable with that feeling. You can introduce this as a fun activity to your group of friends. Make it a point of pride not to know. This will translate into greater comfort about the future and make you available to the vast ocean of creativity that flows from the unknown.

6. Notice details. Wherever you are, examine details with curiosity and interest. There is always something new to discover. Focusing on details keeps the world around you looking and feeling fresh. If it's a location, notice the decor.

If you're with a person, notice what they're wearing. You can comment on it if appropriate. Showing interest brings you closer together. Let the details of the world around you pull you out of your self-absorbed mind and into the aliveness of what's in front of you.

7. Focus on yourself. The tendency to look at what others are doing is deeply ingrained. So much so that detractors of personal development call it selfish. But far from it, getting comfortable being you is what this path is all about. After all, you bring yourself to everything you do. Your environment can only benefit from a more joyful, balanced, radiant, and content you. So focus on yourself with hypervigilance and without remorse. There will come a time when you will want to serve others. Until then, focus on yourself first.

LEVEL 2

"Because"

Welcome to Level 2 awareness. The theme for this level is "Because." Here, you increasingly realize that you are the creator of your reality, and when things happen, they happen *because* of you.

Level 2 is a big deal. The crack in the illusion of separateness and a little more awareness around your thoughts and feelings is enough to invite some life-changing insights. Level 2 teaches you that not only is the world not happening *to* you, but the world you see wouldn't even exist without you. It's *your* world you experience. It's *your* world you live in. It's your filters through which you interpret what happens. No one else sees the world you see but you.

Realizing that your lens on life is unique has far-reaching consequences. You can no longer believe your truth is the one truth. You can no longer insist on your version of reality being the one everyone else should abide by. And most importantly, you can no longer blame the world for how you feel.

Level 2 lessons focus on the connection between how you feel inside and what goes on around you. They make you realize that your inner world dictates what shows up in the outer world, not the other way around. They teach you how to become more sensitive to how your words and actions impact your life experience and that of others. You expand your growing awareness of seeing yourself even less as a separate entity and more as part of the interconnected whole. Each Level 2 lesson is a transformative stepping stone and adds great depth to your being.

LEVEL 2 | Lessons

Lesson 1
THE MIRROR EFFECT

At Level 1, you're completely identified with your thoughts, hypnotized by your beliefs, and unable to witness anything without mentally judging it. Your sense of separateness is all-pervasive, and you constantly struggle to make headway in your search for happiness. Life feels like a riddle you cannot solve.

Starting with Level 2, however, you see a connection between how you feel and what happens around you. When you're in a negative mindset, you experience more negativity. When you're in a positive mood, things work out for the better. At first, you might think it's just a coincidence. But when these patterns keep repeating, you take notice. You start to see the mirror effect.

With time, a more profound wisdom arises that whatever is happening is not happening randomly. It's not happening because that's the only way it can happen. It's happening that way because you see it that way.

In other words, the world you see is a reflection of you. Your moods, attitudes, degrees of optimism and pessimism, expectations, dreams and desires, fears and emotional wounds. The person you are on the inside determines what jumps out at you on the outside. Wherever you go, whomever you interact with, you're always only experiencing yourself.

Initially, you might interpret this mirror effect as hurtful and demeaning. You might think that all it does is show you that you're not good enough and that your misery is your own fault. But that's only because self-blame is a hold-over from Level 1 victim mentality—of things happening *to* you.

Rest assured, making you feel bad about yourself couldn't be farther from the intended purpose. Nor are your perceived shortcomings anything but that: perceived. Life is simply showing you what parts of yourself need work so you can heal and move on to greener pastures.

Level 2 sets the tone that life is a journey that continuously prompts you to grow and become more self-aware. Once this sinks in, shifts are bound to happen. You can loosen your grip on the steering wheel. You can trust that things are happening to help you, not haunt you. You don't need to fear the future. You don't need to fear failure. You're not supposed to be perfect. If you were, there would be no lessons to drive you forward. There would be no journey. There is a growing sense that you are not your woundedness. Even your deepest victimhood is something you can learn to let go of.

Despite these insights, Level 2 life is still extremely noisy. You still prefer clubbing with friends over taking a yoga or meditation class. You still prefer watching the latest hit show with the hot actor over spending time in stillness and journaling about your day. You still prefer a glass of wine over fresh green juice. There is nothing wrong with any of this. It's Level 2 life. Just know, deep down, the seed is germinating that your self-image is self-generated, your hardships reflect how hard you are on yourself, and disappointments only exist because you're dependent on the approval of others.

That said, embracing the mirror can be a scary process. It means looking into the depths of your being. It means facing the fierce inner critic that is part of your mental conditioning and has become part of your identity. It means confronting everything about yourself you may not like or discovering parts you are unaware of. Not just limiting beliefs, but all your traumas, all your demons, and all your darkness need to be unearthed. Every decision you've ever made, and every truth you're invested in must be put under the spotlight and closely examined. Perhaps you've put decades into a career, presuming it would lead to safety, status, or a comfortable lifestyle. Or you've made promises to a love partner who shares your expectations. Going deep down the path of self-discovery means reevaluating all the motivations on which you've built your life thus far.

Once the first cracks in your truth structure form and the light of your awareness gets in, there's no turning back. Gradually, you start dabbling in self-help blogs, listening to wellness podcasts, and reading inspirational quotes on social media. Invariably, you come in contact with metaphysics. Catchphrases like *visualizing success, thinking it into existence,* and *finding your true purpose* pique your interest. You feel drawn to topics like *positive psychology, the power of thought,* and maybe even *the law of attraction.* After all the struggles and disappointments of Level 1, something is stirring deep within. You feel the excitement building that you might be able to *manifest* your best life after all.

And just when you think all this self-help stuff isn't so weird and woo-woo after all, you come across information that touches a wound you carry deep inside, revealing something unhealed you didn't know you had. The ensuing twinge of pain prompts your rational mind to rear its head and say *Stop! This is not for you. You don't need to open this can of worms. Who believes all this spiritual mumbo jumbo, anyway?* You start thinking the old way of life wasn't so bad after all. It's best to return to Plan A, get back to pursuing goals and achieving outcomes, and discard this inner exploration as a brief, one-time excursion.

Of course, you're just delaying the inevitable. Life is relentless in finding a way to turn you inward, even if it has to bring you to your knees. Eventually, unmet expectations wear you down. Or the funds from that comfortable lifestyle dry up. Or your relationship falls apart. Or you're confronted with a health crisis, having to care for others, or dealing with the loss of a loved one. Whatever it may be, if you don't take the time to heal your wounds and fill your voids, life will catch up with you in a rude way. Any blockages you ignore will grow into much bigger issues than if you had faced them early on.

It sounds paradoxical, but the mirror of life reveals your flaws – not because it wants to punish you – but because it loves you. It wants you to come out of your perceived limitations. It wants you to step into your true power and lead an active and fruitful life. Life doesn't benefit when you're misaligned. Nor do the people around you. Unfortunately, the best motivator to get you out of your shell is suffering. Yes, it seems a bit cruel. But we are not here to question God's motives. The fact is that misery is the best way to get you to take action.

Life wants you to be the person you're meant to be. To get there, you must let go of who you're not. You must learn lessons, solve problems, and gain experience and authenticity to serve others. You must embrace the idea that you must first become everything you want to attract. Trust your intuition and trust the timing. You've tried the planning-and-controlling approach long enough to know it doesn't work. There is a rhythm to your life. Make it a priority to live to its beat.

Lesson 2
OBJECTIVE REALITY

Take the same situation witnessed by multiple people at the same time, and you get a multitude of interpretations. Or when reminiscing with friends about a bonding experience that seems too monumental to forget, everyone remembers it differently. Or when you finally confront your parents about issues from your upbringing that affected you deeply, they see it entirely differently or don't recall it at all. Why is that?

You already know that the mind's attention flickers like a candle. Just because a group of people are physically present in the same spot doesn't mean they're paying attention equally. One of them could be worried about paying bills, while the next one just had a fight with their partner, and another is dreaming about their upcoming promotion and how they'll spend the extra money. So when something happens that draws their collective attention, they're coming to it from very different moods and perspectives.

Level 2 teaches you that there's the *objective reality* of what actually happens, and then there's your subjective interpretation based on the filters of your mind. Objective Reality is a baby crying, a glass spilling, or a car driving by. These things happen whether you're there to comment on them or not. When you look at just the happening – without your mental commentary about it - you can see how simple, straightforward, and short-lived Objective Reality is. It comes and goes before you can form an opinion about it.

Experiencing Objective Reality is difficult because the conditioned mind can't let things be. It distorts, ignores, or amplifies every event by filtering it through your personal narrative, isolating it in time, extending its duration, and contorting it into your subjective experience of it. The result is a much more exaggerated story. Considering the objective examples above, a subjective interpretation might sound like *My child is better than yours because it rarely cries. I can't trust myself in the kitchen because I'm clumsy. The world is full of crazy people who should have their driver's license revoked.* You can see how Subjective Reality contains much more noise.

While your stories tend to exaggerate events, they often also downplay them. You might experience a tough breakup, disappointment, or the loss of a loved one and feel ashamed to share your feelings because you think it shows weakness. Perhaps you've accomplished something great but refuse to be celebrated because you were told growing up not to draw attention to yourself.

Furthermore, your mind interprets events from the past like the old *telephone* game, where one person starts whispering a message into the next person's ear. By the time it gets to the last person, the initial account becomes embellished or infused with new elements, eventually becoming an entirely different story. The stories you tell yourself about your life are no different. They take something simple and make it incredibly complicated.

Just because Objective Reality is simple and straightforward doesn't mean it's boring or dull. Or that you're coasting along without any real sense of motivation. Or that witnessing your emotions means you're not feeling your feelings. On the contrary, Objective Reality is intensely alive because you don't distort the experience in your head. You don't endlessly replay the situation, blame others, and gear up to tell your family and friends about what happened *to* you today. The world you experience before you assign definitions is nothing short of spectacular - precisely because it's uncomplicated and focused on continuous creation. You get to be present at the moment when the formless takes shape. You see life happening in high fidelity and real-time, with intense life force permeating everything. Sometimes, it's good to be distracted because the sheer beauty of unfiltered form is too much to handle.

Seeing things as they are simplifies and streamlines all aspects of your life down to the micro level. When a beep goes off in your car, you notice the sound and inspect what it means. When an overhead airplane interrupts your conversation, you pause, wait for it to pass, and then resume. When the waiter brings you a different meal than you ordered, you can decide to try something new or send it back and wait for your original order. When someone cuts you off in traffic, you swerve to avoid a collision and get back in your lane without missing a beat. If you notice your heart beating, you notice your heart beating. If you notice you're tired, you notice you're tired. Life without your judgment of it is simple and fluid.

But implementing it is not so easy. The mind doesn't distort Objective Reality for no reason. It doesn't create this massive collection of subjective interpretations just for fun. It does so because it is obsessed with using every opportunity to validate and reinforce its existing beliefs. Your interpretations are not random. They reflect your fears, insecurities, and worries, as well as your hopes, dreams, and expectations that make up the conditioned stories upon which you've built your identity and worldview. These stories block you from seeing things as they are. The degree to which you are aware is the degree to which you can see life objectively. You don't get there by wanting to be there. You get there by letting go of everything holding you back.

Lesson 3
RELINQUISHING CONTROL

Level 2 marks the beginning of one of the most significant challenges of your journey: relinquishing control. Even if you've heard about it before, you haven't considered it seriously because you've been too attached to your version of life. By the time you get to Level 2, however, you've tried implementing your plan long enough to realize it doesn't work, and there must be a better way. You're ready to make some inroads and let go of control, even if it seems impossibly hard.

Letting go is hard because you've been controlling everything your entire life, not just by manipulating your environment, but by mentally and emotionally judging things as right or wrong, good or bad, true or false, for you or against you. Everything you believe and don't believe lives on your control grid. A massive structure forms that contains everything you've ever judged. Even future events are put on this control grid in the form of expectations and projections. All these truths and untruths are interconnected, forming the Subjective Reality with your identity at its center. Thus, letting go of any one truth has a ripple effect throughout the whole system, including affecting who you think you are. This is why change is so gradual at Level 2. It's scary to let go of yourself.

Ultimately, your constant need for control is your mind's fear of the unknown. It cannot even let the next moment arrive unknown. It needs to put an expectation or prediction on it before it gets here. Even if the prediction is never accurate, a false knowing is more comforting than not knowing at all.

This fear of the unknown is so deep-seated that your mind tries to predict your life to the end. You experience this whenever you enter a new stage of life or even just when celebrating a birthday. With each passing number, you have a truckload of expectations waiting for you. Where did they come from? Well, like everyone else, you've gone through Level 1 indoctrination. Growing up, you become socially programmed to associate every year of your life with certain expectations and conditions. Plus, you continue to live in a mostly Level 1 society designed by people who are deeply in the grips of their own control grid, which they are all too happy to impose on others if it promotes their self-interests. An entire timeline is instilled and continually reinforced by which your life is supposed to happen, including education, career, relationships, children, retirement, any and all achievements along the way, and even when you can expect to leave your body.

Of course, everything has its purpose. The constant comparison of where you are to where you should be creates immense pressure. When your life doesn't match your ideals - and it never does – you experience anxiety and self-criticism. And that's what motivates you to find a better way. It's ironic that you get upset at the thought of not achieving certain things by a certain age, when being upset is what helps you evolve.

Just like going to the gym and starting with small weights, it's best to practice relinquishing control with minor matters that aren't worth the hassle of resisting. This naturally happens as you mature and learn to conserve your energy. But why wait until later when you can let go of control now?

The benefits are instant. When your control-obsessed mind relaxes, it provides breathing room to let in glimpses of Objective Reality. Insights and clarity arise. Experiencing a moment without feeling compelled to judge makes you realize the heavy burden of upholding your truth structure and how deeply entangled your identity is with your beliefs. Level 2 culminates in one of the most important discoveries: When you let go, your life doesn't fall apart. It just unfolds on its own.

Still, learning to relinquish control is a monumental task. You must heal and dissolve all your attachments to people, places, and things. This is an ongoing effort and carries over to Level 3. But the first cracks in the armor happen here. The light of your awareness is starting to illuminate everything you do. Before long, you realize you have no choice but to relent. Unless you want to suffer forever, you must stop complaining and resisting and learn to let go.

Lesson 4
TAKING RESPONSIBILITY

As you internalize that letting go does not mean giving up, you are led to one of the most pivotal moments of your life: It's all up to you.

This is no longer just an obvious surface statement. You feel the truth of it deep inside. You no longer blindly assume that someone else will step in and save you. It's you who must look under every rock and in every corner of your being. It's you who must experience your own chaos, your own darkness, your own getting lost in the labels and definitions of the mind. You must take your own chances, become your own healing force, and leap into the unknown. No one can do it for you. You must take each step down the path by yourself.

This is why greater consciousness hasn't taken hold in the collective, even after thousands of years of philosophy and spiritual teachings. The wisdom any one individual attains cannot be passed along. You cannot become a deeper person simply by reading or hearing about it. You cannot just dip your toe into it and call it a day. You cannot skip doing the work. Each individual has a unique blueprint to discover within themselves. No teacher or technique can do it for you.

Of course, those who came before you can inspire you to find your truth. But, as the saying goes, the teacher appears once the student is ready. You cannot be ready until something inspires you to look within. And that something is usually a good run of old-school suffering.

Again, no one can suffer for you. Inner truth can only be discovered by each person on their own time, at their own pace, in their own way. But it's well worth it. Once it's in place, you have a foundation for life. All the posturing, persuasion, and propaganda thrown about in society means nothing to a person who knows their inner truth. They cannot be swayed to compromise their conscience. They cannot do unto others what they wouldn't do unto themselves. They no longer feel threatened by the convictions of others.

Many people must hit rock bottom before they feel compelled to turn their attention inward and pursue a more spiritually aligned life. For some, alcoholism, drug addiction, and lying on the kitchen floor with a cockroach running over your face are the turning points. Sometimes, negative momentum must run its course before you muster up the courage to do anything about it. Often, superhuman powers only appear when your life is on the line.

But it doesn't have to be that way. Self-help can be something you develop an interest in simply because you're curious about it. Just like some folks enjoy reading history books or science magazines, so can you delve into the countless spiritual works that exist, from Buddhism to the Bible to the ancient Hindu Upanishads, to China's Dao De Jing by Laozi, to the many great Greek philosophers like Socrates, Plato, and Aristotle, to Roman emperor Marcus Aurelius' writings, and of course all the contemporaries between then and now.

Spiritual buffs can enjoy astrology, tarot, numerology, palmistry, and Akashic records readings. Many find human design, gene keys, astro-locality mapping, and personality tests compelling. Healing is a big part of most people's journey. So, if you're looking for an alternative to conventional medicine – which tends to be symptom-focused – there is sound healing, energy healing, chakra healing, crystal healing, craniosacral healing, and long-established modalities like acupuncture, reiki, ayurveda, and many others found in Traditional Chinese Medicine. There is also play therapy, art therapy, essential oils, somatic therapy, and more heavy-weight approaches like hypnotherapy, inner child healing, family constellations, non-violent communication (NVC), neuro-linguistic programming (NLP), and eye-movement desensitization and reprocessing (EMDR). And if you still haven't had enough, you can do breathwork or go to ecstatic dance on Friday nights. There are even standup comedians who specialize in spiritual jokes. The growing volume of spiritual self-help is endless.

But information alone is not enough. Life still has to push you to a certain point, in subtle and not-so-subtle ways, where you are more interested in seeking wisdom than sipping margaritas. So, even without major trauma in your life, something has made you want to look deeper and take responsibility for your life.

Once you take responsibility, you realize the naked truth of your existence: you're born alone, and you die alone. A Level

1 mind reacts negatively to this. It's too dire of a statement to accept. But at Level 2, you see its validity. Everything you see and experience is about you. Everything *is* you. When breakthroughs happen, they're *your* breakthroughs. When upgrades happen, they're *your* upgrades. When the weight comes off *your* shoulders, it's *your* relief, *your* wisdom, *your* power that emerges. Your life is all about you, you, you.

And that's a beautiful thing. You're on a journey to cultivate the highest possible vibration within yourself. That's not selfish. Your vibration is your main contribution to the world, whether you're sitting in a cave or actively putting yourself out there. The vibration you exude is what you give to others. Your highest vibration includes balance, integrity, and self-love. The degree to which you love yourself is the degree to which you love life.

Taking responsibility means learning to live by your inner truth, which sets a massive shift in motion. You become more grounded, contained, and accountable to your conscience. You see the deeper meaning in everything. You embody the profound authenticity and wisdom of someone who lives in harmony with themselves and life. You move from trying to control your environment to welcoming what it reveals about yourself. You accept that life is your mirror, and success depends not on your circumstances, but on what you make of them.

Level 2 teaches you that you are 100% responsible for your happiness, sadness, successes and failures, health, wealth, generosity and humility, wants and desires, and whether you survive or thrive. You learn one of the most important lessons: When you blame the world around you, you stay stuck. When you accept responsibility, there are no limits.

Typically, accepting responsibility is associated with a harder life in which you bear the brunt of the consequences of your actions. But in spiritual terms, accepting responsibility means surrendering to a higher power. Metaphorically, it means letting the greater current carry you and no longer paddling upstream alone. Finally, you can let go of the things you can't control—the outer world—and focus on the one thing you have a say in—how you feel.

The good news is your life is entirely up to you. The bad news is your life is entirely up to you. Either way, your path is a rocky road. But there's no turning back. There's nowhere to hide and nowhere to run. Life will find you everywhere you go and challenge you to assume the great mantle of your highest self. Wounds will have to be healed, stuck energy will have to be released, demons will have to be battled, and who you thought you were will have to burn to the ground. The person you are now will have to die, and there's nothing you can do to prevent it.

Lesson 5
CHOICE

Social conditioning and how it keeps you from recognizing your true self are recurring themes throughout these writings. While it's hard to avoid the conditioning from one's early upbringing, Level 2 is the beginning of realizing that as an adult, you have a choice in what you give your attention to.

You can choose not to consume the news, binge-watch movies, or participate in the latest social trends. You can choose not to consume intoxicants and junk food or stay in relationships with people who are not a vibrational match. You can choose to sit with your triggers and reflect on what they say about you. You can choose to meditate in the evening and go to bed early so you can wake up rested and enjoy a cup of coffee in noble silence while watching the rising sun. Level 2 is about realizing that whatever you choose to give your attention to becomes the content of your life. Your primary task is to choose wisely.

However, given that most of society exists at Level 1, choosing a life outside the socially prescribed path can be challenging. You'd likely associate with fewer people, own less stuff, live closer to nature, and enjoy lots of quiet time. You'd pay closer attention to how much you sleep and what you eat and generally organize your life around a deep commitment to mental, emotional, spiritual, and physical well-being. You'd spend big chunks of your time disconnected from electronics. You'd insist on a much better work-life balance than most companies provide by default. You would speak up when you feel called to, even if that means rocking the boat. And there would be lots of space in your personal relationships to let each other be.

Level 2 represents the beginning of a lifestyle that defies conventional norms. You're likely to encounter constant resistance and the need to explain yourself - that the above are the necessary conditions for you to be the most productive, creative, and reliable partner in work and your personal life. The simple truth is that when you're well-adjusted, everything you do is well-adjusted.

Conversely, when you're suffering, everything you do suffers. If you're tired, stressed, or overworked, you make mistakes, are cranky, and lack passion. You make a lousy employee and disenchanted romantic partner. You keep looking at the time because you don't want to be where you are, no matter where you are. All of this restlessness comes through in your energy and the quality of your attention. It affects everything you do and everyone around you.

People deserve a special callout because they are your primary source of frustration and stress. At Level 1, you're constantly trying to change how others think to match your own views. But the Level 2 mind starts to back off from needing everyone else to be like you. It recognizes that, just like you, everyone thinks their version of the truth is correct. So, why would you believe yours is the only one? You can't fight them all forever, anyway. It's exhausting going through every day insisting you're right and others are wrong. Insistence is resistance. So stop burning unnecessary energy. It's much easier to stop wanting others to be someone they're not and accept that everyone's reality contains their issues and limiting beliefs, which are theirs to work through and learn to let go of. No longer caring so much about what others think frees up vast amounts of vitality and time you can reinvest in yourself.

The more you invest in yourself, the more your newfound ease and lightness spread quickly into all areas of your life. The big turning point is when you no longer blame others for how you feel. You realize nothing is inherently right or wrong, good or bad, for or against you. It's simply your thoughts about things that make it one thing or another.

Level 2 is your invitation to start living the life you want and let everything else go. No more getting upset that you're upset. No more being miserable about your misery. Life is not being mean or conspiring to bring you down. There's no longer a reason to be constantly annoyed. Your quality of life depends on one thing only: choosing to be you.

LEVEL 2 | Reflections

Level 2 represents a huge leap forward in your evolution as two fundamental truths take hold:

First, you've internalized that life is a mirror. Nothing occurs randomly on its own. Even though a million things are happening around you at any given moment, you only see the ones you're focused on. And what you're focused on are the things you look for. And what you look for is determined by what you like and dislike, what you believe and don't believe, and what you fear and don't fear. In short, you only see things in which you recognize some aspect of yourself. There is no sense whatsoever in blaming others for anything. You are the maker of your reality.

Secondly, you've accepted that you're here to learn and grow. That's why life won't leave you alone. It keeps hounding you as long as you feel you're not good enough. It keeps triggering you until you become the fullest, most uninhibited version of yourself. Life is so invested in your success that out of billions and trillions of beings, it has been instilled in you your very own blueprint. Stepping into your truth doesn't just make for a more genuine, uplifted life. It's how you honor your very existence.

With these two truths under your belt, you are ready to face the world in a new, profound way. You see how letting go of fears, attachments, emotional scars, and limiting beliefs broadens your scope and how letting go of expectations and projections opens you up to new possibilities. You sense there is a path you must take, a personal journey that is unique to you and takes you to the depth of who you are. You understand that your inner truth is the way forward.

ME TIME

As you move through Level 2, me-time becomes your most sacred time. Stillness becomes priceless. Pausing to let life breathe becomes essential. Living out of alignment with your degree of awareness becomes unbearable. You recognize and reject victimhood in yourself and others. You smell propaganda and manipulation a mile away. You see the dark, chaotic energy of Level 1 awareness raging around you, and you set increasingly firm boundaries to prevent any of it from entering your energy field. You know when to speak up, take action, step back, or walk away. You feel ready to stand in the power of your true self.

Level 2 compels you to roll up your sleeves and do the work. At the same time, you can also feel the excitement building. After all the Level 1 misery, a bright spot is finally on the horizon. You have hope for a successful and fulfilling life, after all. For discovering your purpose and becoming a more resilient, self-sufficient, and self-loving person. For no longer feeling inferior, helpless, or suffering from imposter syndrome. For no longer doubting yourself and lacking direction. Instead of fearing the future, you start looking forward to it. You relish your growing independence from what the world around you thinks. You can see a time and place when you no longer feel small but are part of something bigger than just yourself.

Me-time also means a change in lifestyle. You become disinterested in the usual mind-numbing avoidance behaviors. Instead of binge-watching reruns or indulging in over-stimulation, you find yourself drawn to yoga classes, sound baths, biohacking conferences, and meditation retreats. You start exploring healing practices and psychic realms you once thought of as fringe or wacko. Existing friends start falling away because you're no longer on the same wavelength. Your dating requirements go from *kind* and *confident* to *spiritual* and *self-aware*.

FOLLOW YOUR BLISS

Never force yourself to do anything that doesn't resonate. Inner work is hard enough. Every insight causes some degree of upheaval in your life. That's why it's important to pace yourself and only pursue what you feel motivated to do. It takes a while to get used to being true to yourself. It doesn't happen overnight. Don't judge yourself if you feel the pull towards the crowds, the consumption, and the mental stimulation. In fact, embrace it. Experiencing everything you feel called to is part of life's design. Whatever you gravitate to contains the lessons you must learn to advance down your path. Otherwise, you wouldn't gravitate to it.

Indeed, for the Level 2 mind, the physical world still holds much allure. It's still the center of your attention and harbors many compelling interests. As always, don't avoid it, but go through it. Lose yourself in your physical senses, in the glitz and the glamour of it all. This is your time to do it. At this stage, you may not be ready to commit yourself fully to the journey of self-realization. And that's ok. There's never anything wrong with anything you do. You'll know when the time comes to go down another road. All roads are part of your path.

Keep living your life and follow your bliss. Falling in love with the outer world is part of the journey to your inner world. Everything you experience outside shows you more of who you are inside. Most importantly, keep noticing the link between what you see and who you are. This is how your sense of separateness shrinks and your connectedness grows.

GROWING PAINS

Always remember that growth is uncomfortable by design – but that it comes from a place of utmost care and love. Everything is driving you toward your completion. Life wants you to be the person you're meant to be. It wants you to break free of your smallness, dissolve your separateness, and let go of control. It wants you to be open to receiving the infinite trust, purpose, passion, energy, and abundance it has to give, that is always available to you, and that is your birthright.

As long as you feel you're not enough, you make decisions based on lack. You keep feeling like you haven't yet arrived. But it doesn't have to be that way. Work on your personal growth and be the change you want to see in and around you. There's no sense in clinging to your comfort zone. You can't stay stagnant forever. Keep growing and stay in motion. Growth is what you came here for, and it's the only thing you can take with you when you leave.

LEVEL 2 | Paradoxes

The journey to leave behind conventional truth and discover a deeper wisdom and meaning behind life continues. The farther you move up the awareness ladder, the more paradoxes you will encounter. Here are the most common ones for Level 2:

PARADOX #1

The harder you push, the farther you get from your goal.

This one is difficult for the Level 2 mind to grasp. You have been programmed to create a goal, roll up your sleeves, and make it happen. It seems logical that the harder you try, the more likely you will achieve the desired outcome.

But the laws of the Universe work differently. If you're having to push hard, it is a sign that you're off your path, and pushing harder only pushes you further away from it. Or when you keep banging your head against the door, not only does it not let you in, but eventually, you knock yourself out. A truly aligned choice would feel very differently. The door would open up effortlessly and invite you in. Once you step through, things happen on their own to support you. You get the feeling that you've been expected.

There's no sense in banging on doors that won't open. Even if you manage to pry it open or break it in, it doesn't get any easier from there. When you experience resistance, take it as a sign to reflect on your approach and consider looking elsewhere. No matter how much you insist on one particular path, you can't know what your path looks like. You can't know anything, period. You might think it's the ideal door, but it may not be. Whatever your head tells you can't be relied upon. Remember, your mind doesn't know you. Instead, look for the door that opens by itself. Let yourself be invited. The path of least resistance is never a straight line, anyway. It's never the shortest distance. It's always the ease with which things happen.

When you're on the path of least resistance, it doesn't just get you to your goal as seamlessly as possible. You get to enjoy yourself along the way, too, which is what matters most. Life is meant to be easy, light, and fun. Your only responsibility is to stop trying to make it harder.

PARADOX #2

Focusing on what you don't want attracts more of it.

This is classic *law of attraction.* You attract that which you give your attention to. So, *not* wanting something is giving your attention to what you don't want. And so get more of what you don't want. To make matters more complicated, the energy of resistance carries a particularly strong charge, bonding you firmly to what you don't want, amplifying the very experience you want to rid yourself of.

Compared to resistance, the energy of attraction is far less developed in most people. That's because the mind is riddled with doubt, fear, and anxiety about pretty much everything. It constantly worries about the unknown, what something means, what others think, etc. It's much easier to resist and keep things away from you than to invite them in and risk confronting your true feelings about them.

That which you give your attention to, you become. It's as simple as that. Once the truth of that sinks in, you will start noticing to what degree you give your attention to things you don't want. All this time, you've been wondering why you're so unhappy. It's because you're focused on why you're so unhappy.

PARADOX #3

The world doesn't seem out of control when you're not trying to control the world.

The mind sees letting go as giving up, as not getting the life you want. That's why relinquishing control is so hard. On one hand, you want to come out of suffering. But on the other, you want life your way. What makes Level 2 so tricky is that you think you come out of suffering if you get the life you want. So you try harder to control things. But the harder you try, the harder you fall.

Again, there's no reason to feel bad. A big part of your journey is getting lost in your mind and experiencing the chaos of your control grid. Your entire physical life is an exercise in feeling stuck, building contrast and finding a way out.

Ultimately, the solution to your issues is always the same: stop focusing on them. As long as you focus on them, they remain activated in your experience. Sure, you can learn to manage poor behavioral patterns. However, maintenance still requires focus and energy, which you could use for more productive endeavors. Realize that your attention feeds the issue, thereby maintaining the charge you must then manage.

You heal when you no longer see yourself as sick. You gain confidence when you accept yourself as you are. Thinking you have a problem is the problem. The world is only out of control because you're trying to control it. Inner peace happens when you stop judging. These insights keep you moving forward.

PARADOX #4

The more you fail, the more likely you are to succeed.

In Level 1 societies, failure is considered a sign of ineptitude and lack of expertise and should be avoided at all costs. Yet, all the great success stories those same societies celebrate—acclaimed entrepreneurs, inventors, athletes, artists, billionaires—emphasize how important failure is and how you learn nothing from your successes, only from when things don't go as planned. Success comes from getting back up when—not if—you fall down.

It's rather unfortunate that honest mistakes are so repudiated. There are some sectors—particularly the startup scene—where failing fast, failing often, and failing forward are encouraged. However, the more established an organization gets, the more risk-averse it becomes. It loses sight of the fact that working under pressure to be perfect creates more physical, emotional, and mental stress at an arguably much greater cost than building a healthy, structured learning environment ever would. Few business and political leaders understand this.

Replace *failing* with *learning* and *learning* with *growing*. Make time to explore and try things out. Don't think of decisions as absolute. Lean into things and see if they resonate. Only then can your inner voice respond. All the things that don't resonate point to the things that do.

PARADOX #5

The more you sacrifice, the more you will be disappointed.

Once again, society tells you to work harder and dig deeper to reach your goals. It tells you that forgoing things you care about is worth it in the grand scheme of things. But this is Level 1 thinking, where everything is based on results that will lead to happiness.

Level 2 teaches you that this is not the case. The more you sacrifice to reach a particular goal, the more you set yourself up for disappointment. That assumes you even reach your goal. But even if you muscle your way through, you've pushed through so much frustration and dismay, you've sacrificed so much health and joy, you've missed out on so many family events, dinners with friends, and going to bed together with your loved ones, that by the time you get to the finish line, the outcome cannot possibly make up for the cost of getting there.

It comes down to this: If you can't enjoy the journey, it's not worth it. Your journey makes up the content of your life. You should never live for goals, ever. You achieve how you want to feel—not by chasing future outcomes—but by doing what makes you feel that way now. *Now* is the only real currency.

LEVEL 2 | Summary

As you can see, Level 2 doesn't get any easier. Major existential lessons are on the agenda, deeply affecting how you relate to yourself and the world. Realizing that life is happening *because* of you and that you are the maker of your reality is a monumental shift.

To master Level 2, you must embrace the *mirror of life* and self-reflect on everything that happens. The more you come out of Subjective Reality, the more you experience the *objective* one. To do so, you must *let go of control* and *take responsibility* for your happiness.

Here are the main skills you develop during Level 2. Check off which ones you've mastered and reflect on the ones that still need developing. You're ready to graduate from Level 2 when:

☐ You realize everyone has their version of reality and that no one's truth is absolute.

☐ You recognize you're always only experiencing yourself.

☐ You've accepted that life cannot be predicted or controlled.

☐ You're aware you have more choices than you think.

☐ You realize it's ok not to follow the prescribed path.

- [ ] You dabble in self-help, even if the thrills of the physical world are still a priority.

- [ ] You experience discomfort being alone but are actively working on it.

- [ ] Me-time is increasingly growing on you.

- [ ] You increasingly spend more time on things you enjoy and less on things you don't.

- [ ] You accept that growth is uncomfortable.

- [ ] You've noticed that pushing harder doesn't make it easier, only harder.

- [ ] You've noticed that whatever mood you're in, you attract more of it.

- [ ] You understand failure means you're moving forward.

- [ ] You've noticed that having to use willpower is not a good sign. It's much better to look for the path of least resistance.

- [ ] You're getting better at setting healthy boundaries and prioritizing your well-being.

- [ ] You're less willing to sacrifice your happiness now for some future outcome.

- [ ] You're ready to take full responsibility for your happiness.

LEVEL 2 | Next Steps

Level 2 is when you start dabbling in mindfulness. While you're not yet ready to be overtly spiritual, here are several things you can implement that are socially acceptable or that you can do in private so your family and friends won't ostracize you for being a weirdo.

1. Notice the mirror. Whenever you feel triggered, first notice where in your body you carry a charge. This pulls your attention from the outside to the inside. Then, instead of casting blame, ask yourself: What *does this situation say about me?* Make a conscious effort to reflect on why you feel like you do. Where does your need for control come from? Why do you want something or someone to be different so badly? Remind yourself it's all about you. Your feelings are here to tell you something. Find out what it is.

2. Practice gratitude. Spending a few minutes daily counting your blessings can make a big difference in your energy field. Genuine gratitude raises your frequency and aligns you with ease, joy, beauty, grace, and light. It also doesn't take up much time and feels good immediately. You can put simple reminders in key places throughout your home, like a note on your bathroom mirror, or associate them with a meaningful object you carry around or wear. Practicing gratitude is the simplest way to come out of a downward spiral.

3. Practice forgiveness. Holding a grudge keeps negative energy stuck and lowers your vibration substantially. That's why letting go of any misgivings about others is in your best interest. That may involve expressing to them how you feel or keeping your distance and processing it out of you. Your journaling routine can be a powerful tool in this regard. Either way, forgiveness is never about them. It's always about you so that you can move forward with your life.

4. Let go of perfectionism. Modern society expects you to perform at the highest levels all the time. Not only is this unhealthy and unrealistic, but it's also contrary to the nature of life. You learn by trying on things for size. Sometimes they fit, sometimes they don't. Learning is the heart of living. Failing means you're moving forward. Everything is always in motion. There is no such thing as a perfect, static state. Consider the following prompts for your next journaling session: *Why am I putting so much pressure on myself? Where does it come from? What can I do to experience less stress and more joy? How do I focus more on the process and less on the outcome?* Let your reflective writing guide itself. As you answer one question, others will appear. Give yourself time and space to write without analyzing it immediately. Do it in a stream-of-conscious style, and let any emotions express themselves fully while you write. Cry if you feel like crying. Laugh if you feel like laughing. Afterward, you can reflect and determine practical steps. Get used to self-inquiry. You'll be doing lots of it for a long time to come.

5. Surround yourself with people who are equal or elevating. Who you spend time with plays a big role in your personal growth. Level 2 is a great time to evaluate if the people, places, and things around you are part of your growth or if they hold you back. Those who never question the status quo and those stuck on the hamster wheel may no longer be a vibrational match, especially if they're unaware they're on one. It takes courage to let go of people, some of whom you may have known for a long time. But gradually, it becomes clear that no one is worth sacrificing your inner peace for.

6. Get used to ups and downs. Your journey is not a straight path. Level 2 is a constant tug-of-war between doing something to get ahead and banging your head against a wall because it's not working. Then, when you relent, something gives and propels you forward. But only after you've exhausted yourself. Slowly, it sinks in that forward momentum doesn't come from pushing. It comes from letting go. Sometimes it's easy. Other times, you have to claw your way forward. Whatever it is, keep forging ahead. The day will come when you look back with pride at how far you've come.

7. Expand your breathwork practice. As described at the end of the Level 1 chapter, this is your go-to mindfulness practice to train your thought awareness muscle. It's so simple yet so powerful. Increase the time you do this to 10-15 minutes daily. More if you feel called to. Mornings are easiest, but evenings are fine, too. Continue to practice at any opportunity throughout the day. You can do it while waiting in line, in the elevator, and even during sports in between points. Opportunities to take a moment and focus on your breath at the entrance of your nostrils are everywhere. You really can't do too much of it. What you put in is what you get out.

LEVEL 3

"For"

Welcome to Level 3 awareness. The theme for this level is "For." Here, life never happens to you, nor does it happen because of you. It happens *for* you. Of course, that's always been the case. The difference is now you see it.

In fact, that's what it means to become more aware. You suddenly see things that were there all along. It's not like there's suddenly something new. Everything has always existed. Now you're just tuned differently. What was previously skewed or hidden by the labels, judgments, and attachments underlying your Subjective Reality is now so obvious you can't believe you didn't see it before. But that's what happens at lower levels of awareness. Your mind's control grid monopolizes your attention, and you're so entangled in surface reactions that you completely miss out on the deeper meaning of life. Starting with Level 3, you're actively working on letting all of that go.

If you think Levels 1 and 2 are tough, navigating Level 3 is extra challenging because you learn lessons that go against the very grain of your conditioning. Everything you've been told about how life works must be let go. All the clinging and resisting, all the planning and predicting, all attachments and beliefs must be released if you want to master this stage. Your entire Subjective Reality containing your identity and worldview must be deconstructed and replaced with... nothing. And that's as scary as it sounds.

Level 3 lessons require you to dig deep over long periods across all areas of life. Most of your life consists of drudgery with short bursts of positive energy and insights. You feel like screaming because you have no idea what's going on. You're helpless and frustrated. No one has the answers, and you don't know what the heck you're doing or whether it's all worth it. All you can do is trust the process. But even learning to trust the process is a process. Repeatedly reaching your breaking point and wanting to give up is normal. So are deeper revelations and downloads when you least expect it. Life continues to nudge you forward, sometimes quietly, sometimes forcefully. Accepting all this is the very first lesson.

LEVEL 3 | Lessons

Lesson 1
ACCEPTANCE

At lower levels of awareness, the mind reacts vehemently when life doesn't happen according to plan. The idea of not getting what you want is totally unacceptable, endlessly depressing, and brings up anxiety, pressure, and desperation. You think you must push even harder and commit more resources to achieving your happiness. You categorically refuse to accept a version of life that doesn't match your expectations.

Starting with Level 3, however, you see a direct correlation between accepting your circumstances and inner peace. You've experienced relinquishing control enough times to know that it's not the end of the world, that acceptance is not about giving up or giving in, and that it doesn't mean rolling over and letting life trample all over you. On the contrary, acceptance is the first essential step in getting unstuck so you can move forward.

Acceptance is about seeing things as they are – i.e., Objective Reality. You stay calm, balanced, and level-headed, and move through each situation efficiently and effectively. You make good decisions from a broader perspective. Because you no longer linger on the past, you are naturally in sync with each new moment as it arrives. And each new moment demands that you experience it fully–no more, no less–to stay in sync.

From this engagement with life unfolding, a natural forward momentum takes hold. Acceptance emboldens you to take action and create the change you want to see. Because if you don't take action, you fall out of sync and revert to staying stuck. It's one or the other.

A life lived in alignment – with yourself and the greater good - requires that you stay engaged. Avoiding challenges and staying in your comfort zone in antithetical to that. At first, it sounds like acceptance is the harder path. But it's actually the opposite. Acceptance is the path of *least* resistance, while wanting something what has already happened to be different is the path of *most* resistance. As the saying goes, *what you resist persists.* By accepting your circumstances, you are bound to move through them.

But despite knowing that, acceptance is still a tall task, even for the Level 3 mind. It thinks by accepting whatever it is you don't like, it becomes permanent. Or more specifically, the feeling you are avoiding becomes permanent. If you look closely, you can tell that what you're actually resisting is not the situation, but your feelings about it.

For example, if you don't have as much money as you'd like, accepting it feels like you are going to be poor forever. Or, if you've failed, accepting it makes you a failure forever. Or if you've experienced loss, accepting it means you will grieve forever. Or by acknowledging your depression you'll be depressed forever. The mind sees everything through the lens of permanence. Acceptance runs completely counter to that.

Energetically, however, the opposite is the case. By accepting you don't have enough money, you no longer reinforce a sense of lack, which opens you up to receiving more abundance. By accepting you've failed, opens you up to learning and growth. By feeling your loss fully, you let the experience deepen you. And by acknowledging your depression, you are no longer identified with it, which takes you out of it. Acceptance is about returning to the natural flow of life with all of its divine wisdom.

Again, if acceptance were easy, everyone would be practicing it. But it contains a strong element of relinquishing control, something the mind abhors. It prefers to go the opposite direction. It thinks that by resisting, there's still a possibility of getting it your way. This, of course, is completely illogical and goes against all laws of the physical dimension. You cannot change things by resisting them. Nothing that's already happened has become undone because you want it to. But such are the distortions and delusions of the mind.

To complicate matters even more, what you think has happened isn't even real. Only Objective Reality is real. But what you've experienced is your subjective interpretation of it. Remember, you're not living in *the* world. You're living in *your* world. That means all your suffering comes from resisting a reality you made up. And that which you would prefer to happen is also made up. None of it is real. All of it is your subjective filters. No wonder you feel crazy when you live in your head.

But, as always, everything has a higher purpose. Contained in this mental madness lies the ultimate growth opportunity. When you notice the reality of the situation doesn't match your expectations, you have a choice. You can continue resisting and perpetuating your misery, or you can accept your circumstances and move forward. Both choices take you to the same place.

Resistance continues to wear you down until it forces you to relent and make peace with it. And when you do – when you reconcile your subjective expectations with Objective

Reality - you become a wiser, deeper person. This path is full of kicking and screaming.

But when you accept, you avoid the whole running-yourself-into-the-ground part. You don't fight life until it forces you to your knees. By accepting *what is,* you skip straight to the *finding peace* part . The sooner you find acceptance, the sooner you can take action and get your life on track.

Ultimately, there is no path forward that doesn't run through acceptance. Level 3 teaches you to leave behind baggage from the past or expectations for the future and focus exclusively on what you can do to move forward right now. In the bigger scheme of things, you don't know what's positive or negative, anyway. All you can do is see what's there, reflect on what it says about you, and decide how to best facilitate the unfolding. You don't grow by resisting life. You grow by being part of it.

Lesson 2
REACTIVITY

The primary obstacle to *acceptance* is your reactivity. In most situations, it's so instant that the moment something shows up, you're already forming opinions and judgments about it. Right or wrong, good or bad, your nervous system is so hard-wired to react that there's no space for you to just let things be. Acceptance becomes a tedious process.

Your reactivity has always been the primary source of separateness between you and your environment, but other lessons had to be learned first before you could be in a position to do something about it. At Level 3, that time has come.

There is a simple yet profound insight that helps you overcome reactivity: recognize that you don't react to the things happening around you—you react to the feelings those things evoke in you. At first, this sounds like it's stating the obvious. But if you look closer, you see the all-important distinction. Grasping this will change your life.

For example, assume someone says something that triggers you. You may get angry and blame that person for making you feel bad. You may be under the impression you're reacting to them. But if you look closely, it's not the person you're reacting to. You're reacting to an unpleasant physical sensation in your body. In other words, your feelings and your reaction to your feelings are two separate things. The anger is the story you put on top of the unpleasant feeling. The feeling by itself is a fraction of the intensity of your overall experience.

With greater awareness, you can discern the line between a feeling – i.e., the physical sensation that shows up in your body - and your reaction to it. You realize your experience consists of 5% feeling and 95% reaction to the feeling. It's because of the reaction part that you try to control your environment to avoid things that trigger you negatively and cling to more of the things that trigger you positively. Ultimately, you're afraid of the intensity of your reactions, not your feelings.

As your reactivity decreases, your ability to engage with your environment increases. You might experience greater empathy and consider other factors, thereby creating a broader context. In the above example, you might get a sense that verbal abuse is what this person is used to, and they're just blindly repeating the pattern. Or perhaps they're in pain, and whatever they say is just a cry for help. Or you yourself are still raw from a recent, unrelated event, and now you're overly sensitive. Whatever it may be, your level of awareness affects how you interpret things.

A simple way to view this is to take another person standing right next to you. Even though they hear the exact same words, they have a very different reaction. Perhaps the words were not directed at them, or they feel triggered differently, or not at all. In other words, you never react to external events. You react to the feelings that result from your interpretation of the event. Essentially, you react to yourself.

Prior to Level 3, you're unaware that any of this is happening. You think you're reacting to your environment. The whole situation is one big emotional experience. And because you're always reacting to something, you become used to having big emotions. Over time, you become convinced that extreme highs are what it means to be human, that insights are found by continuously increasing the stimuli, and that you are doomed to tolerate the inevitable lows. You could say you become addicted to exaggerated emotions.

The main detriment of exaggerated emotions isn't even the immense energy drain and recovery period. It's that you can't hear your intuition. And without your intuition, you lose your primary guidance system. Furthermore, when your entire emotional spectrum is out of whack, your relationship with your feelings becomes confused and dysregulated. That's why sitting still is torture, why difficult feelings evoke anxiety, why not being invited brings about fear of missing out, and why you need to take pics of your breakfast and share them with the world to feel seen. It's all because of your distorted relationship with your feelings. It's why you're uncomfortable in your own skin.

This behavior is not to be taken lightly. The addiction to big feelings negatively impacts every area of your life. You seek out even more intense emotions through sensory entertainment, binge behavior, and intoxicants in an increasingly desperate attempt to avoid feelings you haven't addressed, especially those concerning yourself. You can see how quickly your emotional life gets messy.

Returning to a more natural, balanced level of emotions takes time. Meditation that focuses on body scanning is key. Just as you've been building greater awareness by observing your mind activity, you can come out of reactivity by practicing observing your sensations.

When you first start meditating, your nervous system is still so jacked up from big feelings that it seems impossible to tame the chaos in your head. Trying to cultivate a calm, equanimous mind exposes the rollercoaster emotions you've become physiologically wired for. Beginning meditators are often shocked to find how difficult it is to keep their minds from spinning. Even when you intellectually understand the value of observing your thoughts and feelings, your nervous system takes time to recalibrate and re-wire itself to this new way of relating to your feelings. Thus, changes can be expected to be incremental but permanent.

Coming out of reactivity is life-changing. No longer lingering on what has already happened opens you up to full acceptance, which moves you forward in your evolution. And while it can be hard at first to establish a dedicated meditation practice, it's much harder to keep stewing in reactive juices.

Lesson 3
IMPERMANENCE

Impermanence is a central theme in ancient spiritual teachings and meditations. You may not see the connection yet. But recognizing the impermanent nature of life is the foundation upon which you build your inner peace. All your inner work, from dissolving separateness and coming out of reactivity, to relinquishing control and taking responsibility for your happiness, to replacing resistance with acceptance, contributes to the awareness that life never stands still, and demanding that it does is the source of most of your suffering.

Still, impermanence is a massive challenge for the Level 3 mind. It continues to make everything permanent so it can feel in control. That's what attachments are all about. You don't want things to change, so you attach yourself to them. Attachments provide a sense of stability and control in your life.

But it's all a grand illusion. Life is ever-changing. Moods, mindsets, motivations – everything is always in flux. The wind, the weather, the oceans, the tectonic plates. The Earth's ecosystem is one giant living and breathing organism. And you're part of it. On average, you shed the entirety of your skin every 14 days. Your heart beats around 100,000 times per day. The average lifespan of a human cell is 7-10 years. If you reflect honestly, you're a completely different person than you were five years ago, one year ago, or even last week. There is not a single thing about you that stands still or is permanent. You are designed to keep learning and growing, in all ways, but first and foremost in your awareness.

When you first enter Level 3, the notion of impermanence is a huge downer. The thought that nothing lasts forever, that all things are meant to come and go, and that everything you cherish is destined to leave you, including your own body, is beyond depressing. You cannot imagine that letting go of things you care about could be a good thing. It's much easier to deny and push all that aside and keep living as if your beliefs are absolute, that you can predict the future, and that there will always be a tomorrow.

But right when you've maneuvered certain pieces into place, other pieces you previously arranged start shifting again. And so you spend all your time chasing down the pieces you think will lead to happiness, trying to keep them from falling out of line. No wonder you feel like you can never get it done. You're going against the very fabric of your ever-changing universe. That's part of why you feel like a victim back at Level 1. In fact, the momentum from lower levels of awareness is still quite strong. The lure of thinking you can achieve your happiness looms large, even at Level 3. It doesn't help when society keeps hammering home the message that permanent happiness awaits once you reach the next milestone. And when the joy from achieving outcomes fades, it means there's something wrong with you, not the general approach. And so you keep chasing goals, blindly repeating patterns, taking no time to reflect and realize what a complete travesty it was the last round.

But now that you've reached Level 3, you're no longer quite as married to the idea of permanence. You embrace that life is happening *for* you, so there's an openness to exploring new ways to live your life. You still want happy feelings to last forever, and sometimes, you even want sad feelings to last forever. Your identity is still very much intertwined with certain thought patterns, and everything that fades is perceived as a loss of who you are. But there's enough space around your thoughts to accept that all things in life come and go, that whatever has happened is already gone, and that tomorrow is another day where it all continues.

One of the primary behaviors of enforcing permanence is trying to predict the future. The more you think you know, the more permanent life seems. But if someone asked you outright if you can see into tomorrow, your answer would be: *Of course not. No one can.* If there were a single person on the planet who could, the first thing they would do is go play the lottery.

Yet, despite this clear admission that no one can predict the future, you keep living like you can. And when things happen differently – and they always do – you blame yourself for not predicting better. Again, this is the madness of living in your head. One of the most impactful things you could do to release yourself from suffering is to stop trying to predict the future. It's an absurdly obvious statement when you see it written like this. Yet, most people keep planning out their life ahead of living it.

The absurdity of this approach to life knows no end. You act as if you'll live forever, yet you consume junk food and buy life insurance. You judge your neighbor for spending money on useless stuff, but feel like a loser if you don't do the same. And when you run out of space, you use it to justify buying a bigger house. You invest most of your energy in everything you *can't* take with you when you die and almost none in the one thing you can: your level of awareness.

Big changes happen once you integrate the notion of impermanence into your mental-physical structures. It diffuses the power any one incident can hold over you. Nothing is important enough to warrant upsetting your peace of mind. Beginnings and endings lose their charge. A broader wait-and-see perspective sets in. Others perceive you as calm and level-headed. A profound peace arises from accepting you don't have control and that it's impossible to know how life will unfold. Today's failure could be the key to tomorrow's success, and vice versa. Judging any one moment to be this or that is futile. You increasingly know that you know nothing and that nothing is knowable.

This is when you stop resisting and start collaborating with your circumstances. You look for the lesson instead of blaming the situation. You look for solutions instead of feeling like a victim. You're more comfortable letting things happen than trying to anticipate them. You look forward to tomorrow with curiosity, without anxiety or fear. You no longer feel like you must be perfect because you've realized perfection doesn't exist in a world always in motion. You're no longer willing to sacrifice your happiness now for some future moment that might never come, knowing that even if it does, it's short-lived. Your health and well-being are far more critical than fleeting notions of wealth and social prestige. You see yourself less as a lone warrior and more as a student of life, always open, curious, and with a beginner's mind. You feel less stress because you're no longer chasing outcomes. Instead, you're fully focused on doing things now you genuinely feel connected to. You enjoy me-time, and inner peace is your top priority.

Most importantly, the notion of *good and bad* loses its charge. When good things happen, you no longer amplify them. You realize that clinging to happy feelings quickly turns into the fear of losing them. To experience pure joy, you must be prepared to let the pleasure arise and pass. No more, no less. Objective Reality only lasts for as long as it's there.

Conversely, when *bad* things happen, you no longer think it's a disaster. You know nothing is something forever. You see the continuous nature in everything and how you can't know its impact on your life. Yesterday's success could turn out to be a detriment. What once was devastating could turn into a blessing. You can take this into the absurd by considering that brushing your teeth for five extra seconds ten years ago impacts your life trajectory ten years from now. The point is, everything you judge one way can turn out to mean the opposite, and then the opposite could turn out to mean the opposite again, and so on. So, ultimately, there's no sense in judging anything to be anything at all.

As long as you live in your head, you cannot escape the obsession with permanence. It's just how the mind works. The only solution is to come out of your head altogether and learn to live from your awareness. This is where meditation comes in. By taking time to regularly observe the arising and passing of your sensations, slowly, the fundamental truth about the impermanent nature of life sinks in, and your mind loosens its grip on the steering wheel. Finally, you realize that control and permanence are total illusions of the mind and that you've been miserable this entire time because you insist that they're real.

Lesson 4
LACK

The suggestion that most, if not all, of your behavior is motivated by lack might trigger you. You might feel judged, belittled, or like something is wrong with you. Maybe it activates your inner critic, bringing up feelings of inferiority and not being good enough. Whatever the case, you might feel a knee-jerk reaction to the idea that you're not in control of your decisions and are just blindly acting out what you're missing inside.

On the surface, the reaction is understandable. It can be upsetting to think some of the life decisions you're most proud of are based on woundedness and inner lack. You want to believe you got married out of love, had children to create a happy family, pursued a career out of talent and ambition, and achieved the dream of a house or nice car because you deserve it. You want to feel like someone who's succeeded in all the key areas of life. Someone who's in control of their thoughts and feelings. Someone who's in charge of their destiny.

As you move through Level 3, you realize this is not so. Everything you do on the outside is motivated by something you feel you're missing on the inside. But don't get defensive about it. This lack is what sets the wheels of your evolution in motion. Consciously or unconsciously, you're always manifesting the next set of circumstances that contain the lessons that make you more aware. If you're unhappy, you seek to create circumstances that make you happy. If you have low self-worth, you pursue goals that give you self-esteem. If you didn't feel seen or heard growing up, you look for relationships later on where that is a priority. Not having something motivates you to want to have it. Not knowing what something feels like motivates you to want to experience it.

Again, this is nothing to be ashamed of. You're trying to feel better, and no one can fault you for that. Wanting something you're missing is the most fundamental human behavior. Lack motivates you and drives you forward.

Level 3 is a game-changer because it teaches you to notice when you're driven by fear, the need for control, or feeling like you're not enough. Transcending these low-vibrational, negative motivations and learning to live from a place of integrity, self-love, and inner abundance is one of the most critical turning points in your awareness journey.

You can tell pretty easily if you're acting from lack. Choices made from lack entail some form of emotional expectation. You think achieving the outcome will make you feel _____ (happy, accomplished, respected, etc). If you unpack this, you can quickly see how fickle and messy the whole endeavor is.

Think about it. You're projecting how the feeling of reaching a goal one day can fill the void of how you feel right now. That means your feelings and the cure are out of sync with one another. The only way this approach makes sense is if you commit yourself to feeling the way you do right now until you reach the goal. You're deciding to stay miserable until then.

Even if you did reach the projected outcome, you cannot possibly predict how achieving something in the future will make you feel. Nor can you be sure you'll still feel the void as you do now once you get there. Thus, there is no reassurance whatsoever that the achievement will solve the initial feelings that motivated it.

Furthermore, by focusing on one outcome as the solution to your worries, you're blocking yourself from any other possibilities along the way. You've committed to only coming out of misery if that one particular goal is reached. Any other approaches and options are invisible to you.

Living for the future is pure conjecture and invites chaos, especially when you take into account that life always happens differently than expected. Most of the time, you don't reach that goal. And even if you do, the happiness from achieving it fades again quickly. And you wonder how life got so complicated.

That said, there's no shame whatsoever in manifesting from lack. Something has to give your life structure and all the ups and downs, twists and turns lead back to your true self. Whatever you create is what you need to experience. It's part of the fundamental design to make you more self-aware.

Looking back, you can see how life at lower levels of awareness is dominated by lack. Devoting your life to chasing degrees, slaving away for promotions and job titles, spending your paycheck on fancy clothes and exotic vacations to post about on social media, and saving for oversized homes in prestigious neighborhoods, so you can attract a romantic partner with whom to binge out every night because you're too exhausted to do anything else – all of this is only possible when you feel you're not good enough without all that stuff.

That is not to say you can't enjoy these things as part of living a life of abundance. The issue is that when you manifest from lack, you make your happiness dependent on a world that cannot be controlled. The harder you try, the more you get entangled in the chaos of your control grid. It's a very different experience when abundance arises naturally because you're aligned with your inner truth.

Your inner truth would never tell you to forgo your happiness now in exchange for some future outcome. It would never tell you to overwork and underplay. It would never tell you to numb yourself to your senses. Instead, it would tell you to enjoy things when you have them and let them go when they leave. To use your time for self-reflection and cultivate authenticity. To enjoy the tree's presence and know the tree enjoys yours. To look up to the stars and feel yourself as endless and vast. To support others in their need to feel seen and heard without judgment. To relish time spent alone as much as in great company. To defend your inner peace with rigor. To meet situations with curiosity and acceptance, focus on solutions, and always be respectful, inclusive, and grateful. To spend more time being still and doing nothing, yet feel yourself part of more than ever before. To be vigilant about any information you consume, knowing full well that you become whatever you give your attention to. To welcome each new moment without fear, marveling at the endlessness of creation, the immaculate details, losing yourself in the impossibility of it all. In Objective Reality, lack does not exist.

Lesson 5
MEANINGLESSNESS

At lower levels of awareness, insisting that every situation matches your expectations is your greatest source of friction. But at Level 3, you start dismantling the control grid, and immediately, you feel the relief of no longer having to predict your future. You're so thrilled with your progress you don't see what's coming at you. You think you've learned your lessons. You think you've let go of so much. You think you've put in the time and done the work many times over. You think you're ready to embrace your new life when suddenly, out of nowhere, the most pivotal moment of your existence arrives.

All that self-reflection and letting go of attachments leads to, well, fewer attachments. And fewer attachments lead to less meaning. And as your last remaining beliefs dissolve, you plummet into the depths of the worst feeling ever: meaninglessness.

Level 3 teaches you that life is inherently meaningless, not in the sense of depressing pointlessness, but in the sense of ultimate freedom. On its own, everything just exists as it is, in its natural expression, whether you're present or not. Everything is Objective Reality until a human comes along and assigns it subjective meaning.

Subjective meaning is all the noise in your head. All the concepts, judgments, and constraints you've learned about in your life – what constitutes good and bad, important and unimportant, popular and unpopular, possible and impossible - make up the many narratives you layer on top of the unadulterated happening. Now, the time has come to let go of all that noise. This is why spiritual growth is often called *unlearning*.

Meaninglessness is the ultimate form of detachment. Everything you've done so far in your life, you did it because you thought it had meaning. You were unaware that you yourself had created and assigned that meaning to it. To let go of all those projections is to fall into the deepest, darkest existential hole. And to climb back out, you must slay the grandest dragon of all: your identity. Every last shred of who you think you are must go. Every last detail you've told yourself about anything must be released. Even your deepest-held values must be dissolved.

You don't do this willingly. Nobody does. It's an unspeakable leap of faith to forever leave behind the person you've created and become whatever awaits on the other side. Many spiritual seekers who have made it this far suddenly stagnate, unable to muster the courage to cross this crucial threshold. Their resistance to change is so firm, and their attachment to the form world so concrete that life has to push them to the edge of their wits until they're willing to let go.

Once they do, the ensuing freefall is the scariest thing ever - because it's the end of *you*. One moment, you're leading a fairly normal life, integrated with friends and family, pursuing the socially accredited path. The next, you find yourself sobbing on the kitchen floor, feeling abandoned by life, ridiculed by those closest to you, wondering if this surrender thing is real or if you're just going crazy. You might find yourself confused by a myriad of symptoms, from fluctuating moods and sudden waves of emotion, to physical symptoms like nausea, extreme fatigue, distorted senses, and shooting pains. You might find yourself keeling over, clutching your stomach, grimacing from the anguish of your guts being ripped out by invisible forces. You might curl up in a corner, gripping your chest to keep your heart from exploding. You might find yourself detached and apathetic, with nothing left to cling to or ground to stand on, unable to get up to brush your teeth because it's all so meaningless. Congratulations. You are experiencing your *Dark Night of the Soul*.

The bad news is that *The Dark Night* isn't just one night. In fact, you don't know how long or intense this freefall will be. The good news is there's no longer a ground for you to crash into. Granted, that may not be the reassurance you're looking for. But that's the point. There's no such thing as reassurance. There is no such thing as knowing for sure. There will be no control grid from now on. Up, down, left, right, material, immaterial. Every orientation you've ever known dissolves into nothingness. It lasts for as long as it needs to until no part of you remains that believes anything has inherent meaning. Every last bit of darkness you harbor must come to the light.

Many people experience the early symptoms of this phase as what is commonly called *midlife crisis*. This is when the feeling crops up that the way you've been living doesn't make sense, primarily driven by the realization that you're no closer to the happiness you've been promised than before. In recent times, this experience is showing up sooner in the form of a *third-life* crisis and even a *quarter-life* crisis. Unfortunately, most do not see this through. They run to the doctor, get put on meds, go back to work the next day, and forget all about it. Modern societies are not designed to support spiritual growth. Have you ever heard of any company offering *enlightenment leave?*

For those who surrender to the process, a tumultuous time lies ahead. *The Dark Night of the Soul* period can last from a few months to a few years. Reconfiguring your whole being, your wiring, your energy field, and how you see the world takes time. Everything will be different. Nothing will be the same.

However long it takes for you, be extra kind, patient, and gentle with yourself during this phase. Give yourself the space to get used to the higher frequencies your being is re-calibrating itself to. You're about to turn the corner in your journey, and you need every ounce of energy to get settled in your new skin. It's ok to fall down as long as you get up again. It's ok to feel defeated as long as you ask for help. It's ok to feel lost - finding yourself takes time. But you can no longer resist the divine will. Come hell or high water, your true self will rise.

When you first hear about *The Dark Night of the Soul*, you might be inclined to reflect on your life to identify if such a time has already occurred. If it has, you would know. If it hasn't, you're still in the run-up to it. The greater your resistance to change and the more attached you are to outer form structures, the longer the road ahead of you. That doesn't mean you won't have moments of deep insight along the way. You will. It's just that the final collapse of all meaning has yet to come. But don't focus on that. You can't make it a goal, anyway. Keep working on yourself. Keep growing your awareness. Keep accepting who you are and letting go of who you're not. That's the road that takes you there.

LEVEL 3 | Reflections

Level 3 is a huge wake-up call that the way you've been living no longer serves you, and never has, other than in building contrast that would motivate you to find a better way. Now you're free enough to confront all the main blindspots of the conditioned mind.

THE ILLUSION

In the early stages of awareness, it's all about experiencing the physical dimension. You're fascinated with being human, being in your body, and having sensory impulses. And rightfully so. It's thrilling to have feelings and experience the world around you. There is an endless diversity of living creatures, all animated by some mysterious life force. How amazing is that?!

Naturally, social activities, material desires, and sensual pleasures dominate your schedule. Spending time alone to meditate on life's deeper meaning doesn't. Dancing the night away to bass-heavy, organ-jarring beats is much more appealing than thinking about how everything in life comes and goes. And who could blame you? Nobody wants to be Debbie Downer and point out that it's all an illusion. Nobody wants to wake up from this dream. The material world seems predictable and plannable and promises you guaranteed happiness and success. Why pop that bubble? Why make it hard on yourself by going against the grain? If the grain didn't work, why are most people doing it? The pressure to follow the beaten path is immense.

And just in case there is suffering on this beaten path, there are places you can go to commiserate with your fellow sufferers. Suffering together is a meaningful experience in and of itself. You can attend work parties or sporting events or proclaim solidarity with the latest social movement. Endless opportunities are available to numb out, cover up your aloneness, and pretend to each other that deep inside, you're not unhappy, scared, and lost. The illusion – you tell each other – is to imagine a world without constraints—a life of freedom, passion, and happiness.

Calling the illusory world *the real world* shows how much of society is still working through lower levels of awareness. Consequently, all the rules and structures in place are designed to keep you small, reactive, and lodged in your headspace. This is why feelings of anxiety, boredom, loneliness, and purposelessness are so prevalent. You live in a world that amplifies your mind and relegates your intuition—a world that promotes fear and takes advantage of your sense of lack.

As you move through Level 3, this clash between your high-vibe aspirations and the energies present in general society grows in relevance. You might find it difficult to simply walk down the street, as you can no longer tolerate the energy of violent billboards or the constant call for consumption. You no longer resonate with certain art, music, and entertainment, as the chaotic frequencies of the creators come through in their work. You can no longer stand to hear politics as you see the agenda behind the words. Watching the news feels like an act of self-harm. So do dark movies, foul language, numbing out with food, alcohol, sex, or artificial substances, killing time, attending weddings of people you don't know, hanging out with nay-sayers, dealing with toxic family members, and working a day job you hate. To a Level 3 traveler, the rest of the world looks increasingly insane.

THE WORK TRANCE

Your day job deserves a special mention. This is where long commutes in bumper-to-bumper traffic and endless hours under artificial lights in climate-controlled buildings absorb most of your vitality. Contrived deadlines and promises of promotions keep you focused until you realize too late that your health is shot, your happiness non-existent, and you're still struggling to pay the bills. Either you face getting laid off or quitting outright to recover from burnout. The modern work environment is a collective trance that keeps its participants trapped in a life of drudgery interspersed by happy hours and weekend getaways.

But this trance is just as much a part of your evolution as sitting in meditation ten hours a day. Maybe even more. By the end of Level 3, the contrast from these unsatisfying experiences turns into a burning desire for a more conscious, harmonious lifestyle and being of service to others. What was once an abusive illusion has led you to want something balanced and real. What was once a blind struggle has turned into insight and wisdom. You see? Life works.

COMPASSION

It's a typical Level 3 experience to catch yourself wanting to smack people stuck at lower levels of awareness. Their self-induced and self-sustained suffering has become so obvious to you that you can't believe they don't see it. You quickly forget that – not too long ago - you were one of them. You were part of the madness. And the madness pushed you to become the person you are today. So, everything has its purpose. Once again, the continuous lesson is to come out of judgment and accept the world as you see it wherever you are.

Learning to be compassionate towards those still toiling away at lower levels is a big part of moving up the awareness ladder. Do your best to be understanding, patient, and empathic, and never make anyone feel bad about themselves. Everyone needs to feel acknowledged at whatever station they are at. Feeling heard and seen is what they need before they can move on.

Don't forget to create a safe container for yourself, as well. Everything has a frequency that impacts your mental, emotional, physical, and spiritual well-being. Choose your habitat wisely. Strive to create environments that inspire and uplift you. Your circle of friends should be your tribe, not people you hang out with by default. Your home should be your sanctuary, whether it's a rented room or an estate you own. Design it and organize it as an extension of you. Whenever you leave the house, go with a passionate purpose, not because you don't want to be home alone. Go into spaces because you really want to, not because everybody else is there. Your life should be focused on getting to know yourself better. Make your environment reflect your self-knowledge.

EXHAUSTION

Level 3 shifts are profound but also exhausting. Most of the time, you're tired from all this inner work. You might find yourself longing for the good old days, for a time when things seemed to stand still, even if you were less aware. The saying *ignorance is bliss* comes to mind, implying that when you're unaware, life is easier.

Of course, it's not easier. Firstly, you forget how deeply unsatisfying lower levels of awareness are. There is a low, simmering discontent that won't leave you in peace. You keep waiting for your life to begin. Secondly, just because you're unaware of something doesn't mean it's not there. In fact, that's what it means to be unaware. It's there - you're just not sensitive enough to notice it. Thirdly, thinking like this is useless. There's no sense in wishing you could turn back the clock. You are where you are. That's why the first Level 3 lesson is *acceptance*.

You may also catch yourself complaining about how slow progress is. You wish your healing journey would happen faster and conclude sooner. You want to get it over with and start living the enlightened life. You're so close, you can taste it. But mostly, you just want the anguish to stop. You're tired of feeling exhausted, helpless, and powerless.

But it doesn't stop. It's just that your capacity grows. And this takes time. Once again, acceptance is key to getting there. The whole point of what moves you forward is to learn to accept what is. Ultimately, the future cannot bring you what you lack inside. You can only accept who you are right now and work on that.

Energetically, you must be super honest. You can't cheat the system by practicing mindfulness, but secretly, you have a goal in mind. It doesn't work that way. You can't fake energy. To move effortlessly through an energetic world, you must be at peace with what's happening right now so that you can be energetically free to see the next moment for what it is.

There might also be times of stagnation when you feel discouraged because you're not progressing despite all the hard work. Of course, being ok with feeling stagnant is part of the lesson. You are being tested in all aspects to accept the moment exactly as it is. So, when things slow down, accept it and use it to take a break. Relax and recover while you can. Trust that divine timing is always right. Your next growth spurt will kick in soon enough. Just know you can't move forward by resisting where you are.

REWARDS

No doubt, it's annoying to be constantly pestered by life. You barely get a break. If you don't feel like growing today, life doesn't care. As soon as you work through one issue, the next one is knocking on your door. But there are rewards to this constant push for expansion. Remember why all this is happening. Life doesn't want you to stay small, hurt, and wounded. It doesn't want you to feel helpless, disoriented, and lost. It wants you to heal, grow, and recognize your unlimited nature. It wants you to experience peace and feel at home in your body. It wants you to be whole and recognize your inherent perfection. Level 3 shows you how life is designed with your utmost well-being at heart.

Once you internalize this dynamic, you cannot help but love life. You cannot help but trust divine timing. You cannot help but feel increased confidence. You listen less to outside voices and more to your inner one. You know your strengths and the parts you need to work on. You support others in seeking their own truth because you want them to feel anchored in themselves like you are. You experience an entirely new level of acceptance of self and no longer need to impose your opinions on others.

You're also more productive than ever before. Not just because you're calmer and more focused, but imagine getting all that time and energy back from being lost in thought. Imagine how much more you can explore and accomplish when making decisions with clarity and presence. You now have the wisdom to enjoy the process, regardless of the outcome. You have the inner strength to prioritize things you love doing over things you're supposed to be doing. And you have the humility to realize your whole life has been a collection of subjective stories. You know the solution is not just telling yourself the right ones but not telling yourself any at all. There is a world waiting beyond your stories that is so vast, so limitless, so magical, and you're ready to live in it.

LEVEL 3 | Paradoxes

Level 3 paradoxes are increasingly subtle yet more profound. You have to take them to heart in a whole new way. It's not uncommon to realize there's a new level of refinement possible or a new approach to life you've missed thus far. You realize there's always a deeper level you can tune in to. The work never ends, truly.

PARADOX #1

You don't calm a busy mind by wanting it to be calm. You calm it by accepting that it's busy.

This is the quintessential frustration for beginning meditators. Naturally, you think the goal of meditation is to calm your mind. You sit down with that goal in mind. You might experience bliss in your practice. But when you do, from that moment on, getting back to bliss becomes the goal. It's like you can't help yourself. That's because your mind still cares about setting goals, a tendency that goes back to Level 1 programming. But now is the time to accept the Universe doesn't work that way. Wanting your busy mind to be quiet doesn't make it any more quiet. If anything, it makes it even busier because you're so agitated that it's not following your command.

The solution is always to accept whatever state your mind is in. Acceptance calms it down, while resistance keeps it restless and jittery. Your thoughts are the best opportunity for practicing acceptance. If your mind is busy, it's busy. If it's calm, it's calm. The better you accept your thoughts, the better you accept the reality around you. Remember, most of your suffering comes from wanting things to be different than they are.

PARADOX #2

Your job is not to make yourself happy.
Your job is not to make yourself unhappy.

Your natural state is to be happy and high-vibrating. But you lower your frequency with all that planning and pursuing, all those attachments to thoughts and feelings, all that judging of yourself and the world. Everything you give your attention to carries an energetic weight. Even positive energy is a weight. By no longer reacting, you don't take on the weight, which automatically raises your vibration and returns you to your natural, happy state.

The challenge is that your mind sees it the other way around. It compels you to create a plan and execute it. In hopes of finding happiness one day, you sacrifice your joy now. You are so focused on becoming happy that it reinforces your being unhappy.

Once again, your happiness is not found in outcomes and goals. It is found in acceptance of who you are and where you are right now. There is no shortage of *right now*. You never have to go looking for it. It presents itself to you constantly and continuously. All the ecstatic experiences you seek to find yourself in, all the big feelings you live for, and all the milestones you hope will fulfill you are not special at all. Nothing is more powerful than being at peace with yourself right now. That's what moves you forward. Nothing else.

That doesn't mean you shouldn't seek out new experiences. It just means finding contentment every step along the way. When you don't need the next moment to be something, you're much more likely to enjoy whatever comes. Happiness does not depend on your circumstances anyway. On the contrary, happiness is freeing yourself from the world around you.

PARADOX #3

Thinking you have a problem *is* the problem.

You've heard it before. You become that which you give your attention to. If you keep focusing on something being wrong with you, you keep feeling like there's something wrong with you. When you don't feel like there's something wrong with you, you don't feel like there's something wrong with you. It's that simple.

But there IS something wrong with me, your mind tells you. That's the challenge right there. You're identified with the problem. Once identified, it's hard to let go of. This is where many Level 1 parents, teachers, therapists, doctors, politicians, etc., do you a huge disservice because they imprint this victim identity upon you. You then tell your family, friends, and coworkers that you have this or that problem. The collective belief then reinforces you feeling like a problem.

This is what happens in a low-awareness world. It's hard not to get sucked in. You must learn to navigate your circumstances with complete irreverence toward so-called experts. They could have the highest accolades and decades of experience under their belt. Yet, if all they do is regurgitate Level 1 thinking they themselves are programmed with, it could be a terrible match for you. Always sort out who aligns with your level of awareness and who doesn't. Don't worry, it's not hard. As long as you use your intuition, you recognize them right away.

PARADOX #4

Figuring yourself out is a rejection of self.

When you first embark on your journey, you might be inclined to feel like the awakening process is about figuring yourself out. But this is not so. Because as long as you're figuring yourself out, you haven't accepted who you are. Many people become lifelong experts at figuring themselves out. They will seek out the best teachers, the most powerful shamans, spend hours sitting in rigid stillness, chanting endless mantras and ohms, and travel to the farthest corners of the planet to visit ancient holy places where the masters once walked, only to realize – if they're lucky - that *figuring yourself out* was just another sneaky way of living for outcomes by not accepting who you are.

The only way to live a healthy, happy, and inspired life is to stop figuring yourself out. When you stop wanting to be different, you stop running away from yourself. Accept who you are now. From there, life will evolve you on its own and in perfect timing.

PARADOX #5

You change others by not wanting them to be different.

The most significant source of friction is other people. You want them to think like you, walk like you, talk like you. Deep down, you want them to be you. But that's only the case when you live in your head, defending your truth structure. You want the people around you to validate your existing beliefs.

When you learn to live by your inner truth, however, you can let others be. You allow them to feel seen and heard without judgment. You have the emotional intelligence to recognize the experience they're seeking to have and can hold space for it. You grow people the most by letting them grow. Anything else is interfering with their journey. When they no longer feel your resistance to who they are, they suddenly have the freedom to self-reflect and hear themselves speak and think. When you no longer feel the need to impose yourself on others, everyone flourishes.

LEVEL 3 | Summary

You can spend an eternity at Level 3. There is so much to learn about yourself. Plus, all this inner work is not easy. It takes courage and discipline to get through the upheaval. But something inside is pulling you towards your true self. Now that you understand life is happening *for* you, you sense the golden opportunity to live your best life after all.

To master Level 3, you must accept things as they are without wanting them to be different. Recognizing the impermanent nature of life is a big part of that - not just intellectually - but by internalizing it through your continued mindfulness practice. Becoming aware of any lack that might be motivating you is also key to letting go of old stories and limiting beliefs. And if you do all that right, you are rewarded with a plunge into meaninglessness and a total collapse of your Subjective Reality. Fun!

Here are the main growth areas you develop during Level 3. Check off the ones you've mastered, and reflect on the ones that still need attention. You're ready to graduate from Level 3 when:

☐ You understand that acceptance is what moves you forward, and resistance keeps you stuck.

- You've internalized that life is always evolving, always in motion. There is no life you can create that will forever stand still. Nothing is permanent.

- You recognize that most of your previous decisions – some big, life-altering – have been motivated by lack.

- You recognize that life is inherently meaningless and that this is not a bad thing. On the contrary, it gives you the choice to design the life you feel called to live.

- You no longer judge those at lower levels of awareness. You have nothing but compassion.

- You've learned to use the slow growth periods to rest and recharge.

- You trust divine timing.

- You're focused only on the things you can control. Chiefly, you've stopped making yourself unhappy.

- You're aware that you can't think your way out of overthinking.

- You've recognized that the best way to change others is to be the change.

- You're aware when your mind is busy and know how to quiet it.

LEVEL 3 | SUMMARY

☐ You're committed to self-development as the central theme of your life. There's always some activity or event you're signed up for.

☐ You're actively setting and re-setting healthy boundaries with friends and family.

☐ You notice your circle of friends is much more fluid. Some leave, while new ones enter.

☐ You're no longer frustrated at the slow pace of your progress. You've accepted that it takes as long as it takes.

☐ You're way more patient. You allow situations to unfold over longer periods before assessing them.

☐ You're rarely absent-minded.

☐ You're no longer anxious about your future. You look forward to seeing what happens next.

☐ You no longer live for outcomes. You only pursue things as long as you enjoy the process.

☐ Self-care has become a central part of your life.

LEVEL 3 | Next Steps

Level 3 lessons must be taken very seriously. Otherwise, you can keep looping for a very long time. And even that is ok. But why suffer more when you can suffer less? Why not move through it sooner if you can? You still have a choice in all this. Here are some practical steps to guide you through Level 3:

1. Practice self-reflection. Whenever you find yourself in a difficult or uncomfortable situation, ask yourself, *What does this say about me? What is the lesson?* Doing that means you no longer resist or judge what's happening. Instead, you experience the situation from your awareness.

2. Think of acceptance as temporary acceptance. Whatever happens around you, see it as a temporary configuration of elements, not a cemented truth. Feel whatever comes up at the moment, but develop the reflective perspective that tomorrow is another day, and you'll see how things look then. Even a brief moment of temporary acceptance can introduce enough space into your thoughts for the mind to let go. When this happens, you move forward. And moving forward is the first step to creating positive change.

3. Be intentional. Bring a new level of intention into everything you do. Let go of the notion that one thing is more important than another. Brush your teeth with as much precision as paying your bills. Give the supermarket cashier the same quality of attention as your boss. Listen to a stranger with as much respect as your partner. A big part of transcending the judging mind is experiencing everything as equal.

4. Spend more time alone. If there's one thing that can improve your life, it's more alone time. Alone time provides critical insights into your relationship with yourself. This also means facing difficult feelings, uncovering unhealed trauma from your life and from your lineage, and confronting the unlived life of your parents. One can understand the tendency to look the other way and keep one's head in the sand. Healing is hard, but never as hard as living with false, self-imposed limitations.

5. Treat your environment as an extension of you. Whether you live in a rented room or a mansion, energy doesn't know the difference. The frequency of your physical environment can help you expand or stay small. Make your space your own, and it will strengthen your spiritual metamorphosis. Always be ready to reorganize and upgrade based on who you are now. Make your surroundings match the highest vibration possible.

6. Update your boundaries. It's important to continue to redraw boundaries to support your expanding awareness. Setting new boundaries with family members, condensing your circle of friends, and limiting your social activities can go a long way in being true to the new you. Also, create more space at work, for instance, by asking your employer for more flexibility and working remotely more often. Or perhaps you're done with all that and are ready to move to the countryside, start a homestead, or quit your job and become an expat in a foreign country. Whatever you decide to do, always trust your inner voice. It's your only ally in a crazy world that thinks you're the one who's nuts.

7. Start doing. The most important thing is to start doing. Doing is way more important than thinking it through. It's too easy to get lost in the big picture. Thinking usually leads to feeling overwhelmed, and you never get off the couch. Whatever you want to create or pursue, lean into it and get a taste of it. Make it real. To truly know if something resonates, you must feel it. You can always back out again. Drop your predictions and pre-dispositions and experience the Objective Reality before making a big commitment.

8. Create small wins. Start your day with small wins to build positive momentum. Ultimately, a win is a win. You can feel just as satisfied folding your laundry or taking the trash out as you can meeting a big deadline. Look at your existing routines and identify small tasks to turn into wins.

Even brushing your teeth or taking a shower can inspire a sense of completeness and accomplishment when you frame it that way. Also, it's important to end the day on a win and take that feeling into your sleep. Use journaling to help you evaluate and track what works best for you.

9. Maintain a learning mindset. Life is your teacher, and you are the student. As such, view life as a journey of endless learning opportunities. Maintaining a learning mindset keeps your energy field open and in receiving mode. That doesn't mean you shouldn't celebrate wins and achieving milestones. Just realize they are brief snapshots of the bigger, unfolding adventure. Everything must be allowed to happen in all of its dimensions. You're ready to ascend to the next level when all is possible.

10. Keep doing breathwork. Continue to build your awareness muscle by noticing your thoughts. Keep creating a bigger gap between you and your thoughts so you can choose which ones to engage in and which ones not. Increase your practice to twice a day for at least 15 minutes each. Mornings and evenings are best. Also, keep integrating this practice throughout your day. Look for new moments in your existing routines.

11. Start body scanning. Add body scanning meditations, such as Vipassana, to your daily routine. Start with 15 minutes in the morning and evening immediately following your breathwork sessions.

LEVEL 4

"Through"

Welcome to Level 4 awareness. The theme for this level is "Through" because when you no longer get in your own way, life starts flowing *through* you.

In the wellness community, there is much talk about healing but little about what life is like once you move beyond your wounds. It's understandable, given that most people are working through lower levels of awareness, where short-term relief is more important than long-term vision.

But what a vision it is. Level 4 elevates you to the highest, purest vibration yet. It teaches you to release any remaining resistance to yourself and life. Here, you learn to let your thoughts and feelings flow through you freely. Your inner voice becomes loud and clear. You become fully committed to mindful living, a clean lifestyle, and shielding your energy field from low frequencies and dark forces. You fully embrace your spiritual nature, leaving aside distractions that don't serve you and surrounding yourself with people, places, and things that do.

Level 4 lessons feel less like challenges and more like opportunities to step into your power. You've reached the tipping point in your journey, where you go from suffering separately to continuously connected. The time has come to harness your infinite nature and live purely by your inner truth.

Once you do, a life of clarity and purpose unfolds. Of finding beauty in the littlest things. Of seeing perfection in simplicity. Of being at peace with yourself and the world, no matter what happens. Of trusting the greater current to take you where you're supposed to go. And of unlimited abundance. Level 4 feels like you've finally arrived. It's the moment you've been waiting for. It's not the final destination, but it's close.

LEVEL 4 | Lessons

Lesson 1
PURE PRESENCE

By now, you're aware of the importance of staying present. Presence is the bedrock of most spiritual teachings from ancient to contemporary times. At lower levels of awareness, presence continues to elude you, primarily due to the ongoing distractions and noise in your head. At Level 4, however, all that is about to change.

Level 4 teaches you that presence is not a state to be achieved. You are always present at any given moment. In fact, it's impossible not to be present. Everything that exists *is* present, and everything exists *in* presence. Presence is all there is. Even when you're lost in thought, you are lost in thought right now. So it's never a question of whether you are present or not. It's a question of *what you are present with*.

You can be present in one of three ways:

1. You can be present with life unfolding in front of

you - but *without* judging, labeling, or otherwise engaging your mental structures. This is when you're a silent witness to what's happening. Your mind is quiet and you purely see things as they are – call it *pure presence.* Pure Presence is a smooth, continuous experience of one moment fading into the next. It's like acceptance on steroids. You're not just accepting things after they show up and once you've assessed them. Rather, you're already in a state of acceptance when they arrive, so you never judge things to begin with. Instead, you're welcoming life, ready for it to happen, without a hint of fear or trepidation. Whatever shows up, you see what you're actually seeing, hear what you're actually hearing, smell what you're actually smelling. You're completely tuned into your senses, neither adding nor taking away from it.

2. Next, you can be present *with your thoughts* about what's happening in front of you. That means there's a layer of interpretation between what is happening and what you see happening through the cognitive veil of your mind. This may seem like a completely normal way of operating. And, granted, it's not the most agonizing state to be in. At least you're thinking about things that are actually happening, which keeps the mind chatter relatively contained and prevents you from going too far

down rabbit holes. The issue is that as long as you intellectually interpret what you're seeing, you're not actually seeing it. You're seeing a skewed image through your mental filters, i.e., your Subjective Reality.

This is the type of presence you cultivate at Level 3, where your main goal is to keep your mind from wandering to random things and focus your attention on what's in front of you. You might get glimpses of Pure Presence, which will be explained in the next chapter. But most of the time, you're struggling to keep your monkey mind under control.

3. Lastly, you can be present with thoughts about random things unrelated to the now. Naturally, that means thinking about the past and future. You constantly replay what already happened and try to predict what happens next. Needless to say, this state is full of chaotic, conflicting energy. It is a huge time and energy suck and is the main detriment to your health and happiness. Your whole life is consumed by dealing with thoughts about things that aren't real, but you make them real by believing them.

   This type of presence is most prevalent at Levels 1 and 2. That's when you run through life hypnotized. You blindly repeat patterns, hardly ever wondering why the same things keep happening to you. You're oblivious to the mirror of life and the lessons contained in each situation because you're rarely ever present with the situation. Instead, you're present with thoughts about random things that have no bearing on your life and only make you more miserable.

Many people struggle with the concept of presence. They have a hard time first grasping and then implementing it. That's because presence is foreign to the mind. Your mind loves the past and future - the virtual canvas of its control grid - and reacts almost violently to any attempt to focus on the present moment. But you can see how presence is actually quite easy and uncomplicated. It's simply what you give your attention to.

To provide a more tangible, practical definition, think of being present as the sliver of time when something enters your field of attention and exits again. More specifically, the start of the present moment is when your senses pick up something from your environment, which the brain interprets and converts into feelings arising in your body. And the end of that particular present moment is when that feeling subsides, and everything starts over with the next thing you give your attention to.

You can practice this on any object around you. Look around and find something to focus on. It can be a chair. Look at it, and notice how it makes you feel. If you're looking at it and feel nothing, you're not really looking at it. So, try again. This time, *really* look at it in detail. Notice its shape, colors, and design. Notice its features and the mix of materials. Notice if it's stylish or more utilitarian, beautiful or plain. Do this for one minute before reading on.

Now, notice how the object makes you feel. Perhaps you appreciate it more or even feel gratitude that it's in your life and has served you well. Perhaps you remember how it came into your life and the people associated with it. Or how it filled a role in your environment that was missing. If you do the exercise right, you cannot help but experience feelings in response to being present with the object. You recognize the aliveness in the object, thereby recognizing the aliveness in yourself.

This is when you realize how connected you are to everything. Everything is energy, including you. The more you give quality attention to the world around you—the more you notice the details of even the simplest things—the more you feel your connection to everything that exists.

Labels and definitions make you lose your concentration and connection to the fullness of life. Your mental evaluation of what you perceive takes over, leaving you with a truncated experience. But when you come out of your thoughts and actually are present with something, it comes to life. You come to life. Even if you realize you hate the chair, there's something beautiful in that. By becoming more aware of the chair, you've become more aware of yourself.

Pure Presence allows you to flow freely through the world without interference from subjective interpretation and enjoy the inherent richness of everything that exists. It's a clean, judgment-free, end-to-end process in which your mind decodes your sensory inputs into physical sensations, the resonance of which is then delivered as intuitive wisdom. It's pure throughput from the miracle of your environment to your higher self.

Additionally, because mental labels and definitions no longer consume you, you are free to take in the energy of the situation you're observing. This energy conveys much more information than even a clear mind could discern. Energy bypasses the senses-to-sensations signal chain altogether, and you communicate directly with what is happening through energy channels. Energy is always the most accurate because energy doesn't lie.

While your mind is calm in Pure Presence, thoughts may still arise. However, the quality of these thoughts is very different from those arising from your subjective filters. The mind is motivated by fear, lack, and control. So, thoughts generated from there contain the frequency of those elements. But thoughts arising from Pure Presence are non-judgmental, non-comparative, and don't contain your sense of self. This isn't some esoteric magic. It's simply the result of the quality of your overall makeup. Thoughts arising from mud are muddy. Thoughts arising from equanimity are clear. They arise after taking in the whole situation in a way that honors the continuity of life. There is a spaciousness and curiosity about you because you're not reacting to individual elements as you would have at lower levels of awareness. Instead, you take your time simply observing. Bystanders might perceive you as endlessly patient, receptive, and nonjudgmental.

The best indicator that you've lost Pure Presence is to notice when you're stressed. Stress is an indicator you're experiencing time and are drifting into thoughts about the past and future. To counter when you notice yourself stressing, focus on something extremely detailed, like the touch of your breath at the entrance of your nostrils. That's right. The exact same exercise you've been doing in your breathwork meditation. It's the simplest, quickest, and most powerful way to reconnect with the now.

Lesson 2
FLOW

Level 4 flow happens when you are continuously in Pure Presence, completely in sync with the arising and passing of each new moment. You see things as they are and respond to them as they happen. You no longer assign your own meaning. Instead, you let life connect the dots for you. Thus, you don't need anything to be different because everything is perfect as it is. You also no longer believe in beginnings and endings, so you don't feel tormented by time. In fact, you no longer believe in anything. You have learned to let life be, and you trust if there's a reason to act, you will feel called to it.

Living in the flow is a huge jump from lower levels, where you're always chasing outcomes, compelled to fit everything you encounter into your control grid, unaware that you generate resistance to Source energy whenever you mentally judge something as *right* or *wrong*. It doesn't matter how much social acclaim or material success you have accrued. Your level of awareness is the central determining factor of how you experience the world and, thus, your quality of life.

Even for top athletes who are more embodied than anyone, being *in the zone* is rare. For the most part, they, too, are in the iron-clad grip of their domineering mind. That's why Level 3 acceptance brings so much relief.

However, once you get to Level 4, you move beyond mere relief. With acceptance firmly in place, you're more present more often, tuned to the moment of unfolding. Your whole life starts to flow.

A heightened sensitivity to energy plays a prominent role in your ability to flow. It's no longer a surface, cursory understanding. It's a recognition that everything is energy. Your body is energy. All your thoughts and feelings are energy. All animate and inanimate objects are energy. You are an energy being living in an energy universe. It's an entirely new way of relating to the world.

Suddenly, you see how simple life is meant to be. How straightforward every situation is. How nothing is a problem. Everything is just life happening, and you're a participant in it. And then, without lingering, you move on to the next moment. Earlier in your evolution, you might think that by no longer reacting, life would be boring. But actually, you get to experience so much more. New content pours in faster than you know what to do with it. Your threshold of what is worthy of your attention heightens dramatically. Nothing is clouded. Everything is in high resolution.

The world of old – if you even think back at all - seems utterly complicated and burdensome. Everything is distorted, muted, or amplified. It feels hurtful to be out of alignment with your truth and go against your conscience. Your thoughts, your way of being, everything feels crowded. In contrast, your newfound energy awareness gives you a much broader perspective. You see things from multiple angles, with deep, intuitive insights into the greater energies at play. Your physical senses are heightened, too, as if you've switched to a higher-fidelity bandwidth. That's because you have.

When you're in the flow, there is no noise. Just the silent power of the greater current carrying you on its mighty wings. In this state, you feel like nothing is missing. You naturally lean towards a minimalistic existence with fewer complexities. You recognize physical belongings weigh you down and that ownership is a deeply embedded attachment that fortifies a sense of permanence and control. You're no longer distracted by things that don't resonate and exclusively focused on things that do. You make choices based on what's best for the situation because you and the situation are no longer separate. You are acutely aware of your connectedness to everything and perfectly comfortable with the unknown.

Most significantly, you see universal truth in everything and recognize flow as divine guidance. You act clearly and execute effortlessly without overthinking or second-guessing yourself. You move through the world with utmost curiosity and delight. There is no delay in how you experience life. Everything is instant. Thus, it feels like things fall into place on their own, and you're just acting out your part of a script. When one door closes, another one opens. You can feel greater forces at play, and only a full-body *yes* deserves your attention. Your life is tuned to your passions, and there is no confusion because living your truth has become the norm. You're unafraid of being still, with no sense of urgency to get anywhere. Yet, you're more productive than ever before. Experiencing flow is the most beautiful thing. It's the nirvana you've been waiting for.

Still, you must be mindful. It's easy to get excited when you see things lining up for you and start thinking you're in control again. Before you know it, you've shut down your flow and have to build momentum all over again.

The trick to staying in the flow is approaching life from the other end, from nonjudgment, nonattachment, and nonreactivity. From there, your life flourishes, and your awareness expands.

Ask not what you want from life but what life wants from you. Let it take you by the hand and pull you into the unfolding. Life is designed to guide you all the way – from a blind beginner fascinated with the physical realm to an enlightened master ready to transcend to other dimensions. You don't get there by wanting to be different. You get there by accepting yourself as you are.

Who would have thought it would be so difficult to experience life without constantly judging it? Who would have guessed that *seeing things as they are* is the hardest thing ever? Why cling to your filters when Objective Reality is the most natural thing in the world? You've come all this way and have done all this work to get to Level 4, only to discover the simple secret to a happy and fulfilling life: go with the flow.

Level 4 teaches you that compromising flow is never worth it because you're compromising yourself. The outer always flows from the inner. So, if your flow fluctuates, some part of you is in resistance. Only when you're at peace within can outer peace take hold. Only when you love yourself can you feel the love around you. Only when you embrace abundance are you ready to receive. Once you can hold everything in your energy field, you can manifest anything you want.

Lesson 3
MANIFESTATION

Starting with Level 4, you're no longer motivated to create from inner lack. Instead, what you manifest is derived from your connectedness to life. Insights, ideas, and opportunities come to you, infusing you with endless inspiration, originality, and vitality. Being in the flow is the engine for continuous positive manifestation.

When you're present at the moment of life's unfolding, you can't help but be a master manifester. You can't help but see things clearly, take clear action, and harvest clear results. Source energy is powerful and serene. It pumps formless energy into you and through you for you to give shape to. Your primary challenge is to keep your vessel optimized to capture all that throughput promptly and effectively. It's from this place that you create your life's work.

You may not be able to take on every single idea you download. And that's ok. No longer do you live with a scarcity complex. If not this, then something even better. Always evaluate what you feel called to manifest, whether it's the right timing, if you have the right resources, etc. Finding out if you're ready is not a mental evaluation. You must lean into it and explore. Exploration is a key component of the manifestation process because that's what manifestation is: a process. Manifestation is never just thinking about something and then sitting back, waiting passively for it to happen. When you do nothing, nothing happens.

Even if you feel good about an idea, you should still lean into it to explore it more. You want to feel if it resonates in your body. You want to let the fullness of the idea grow and reveal itself in co-creation with you. You know you're in your head when you keep wavering, getting impatient or frustrated, overwhelmed by the big picture, or talking yourself out of it. Your inner knowing is different. It says *it may be challenging, but I'm doing this.*

The best way to tell if something is your true calling is to examine your motivations. Mental conviction is always driven by lack, fear, or attachment to outcome. Those are the levers of the mind. You think doing X will lead to Y. Your true calling feels very different. It contains the elements of surrender, responsibility, and growth, none of which is very comfortable. Your true calling is the accumulation of all your struggles. No wonder you don't want to be reminded of it. But at this stage, you've accepted yourself and are ready to take that final step into your truth.

Whatever you manifest, the initial spark must be divine. From there, be prepared to be persistent and resilient. After all, you're transforming the formless into form. This is no trivial effort. All your human skills and experience come into play, which is what made you the ideal receiver in the first place.

You never have to fear that your idea will be stolen. Everything you create carries your energetic fingerprint. The life you've lived is like no other, and that life is infused into your creations and makes them unique from any other. You don't own ideas, anyway. Everyone pulls from the same formless cloud. Your only task is to decide to take it on and then honor your commitment.

Once you commit, it becomes your baby, and babies need love and attention every waking moment. It's your duty to see it through. If you let it down, you let yourself down. If you leave it unfinished, you leave some part of you hanging. Whatever idea you take on becomes an extension of you.

Furthermore, it is essential not to delay execution. Your being keeps evolving, and you won't be who you are now forever. Whatever is coming through you is doing so because of how you're currently tuned. If you wait too long, your tuning changes and you're no longer the appropriate receiver to bring it to fruition. You might be a suitable receiver for other ideas, and hopefully, you will act in sync to see those through.

Giving shape to the formless is no small task. The physical dimension is a flurry of scattered energies that are difficult to align. There are many moving parts, including market conditions, financial considerations, geopolitical realities, your skill set, and the level of awareness of the people you collaborate with.

That doesn't mean you should ever let these factors hold you back. On the contrary, you should embrace external conditions because constraints help shape your idea. They provide the real-world context so that whatever you manifest is done in a functional, integrated, and sustainable way.

Ultimately, obstacles are crucial helpers. They are the ingredients that keep ideas fresh and challenge you to dig deep. If everything were easy, there would be no challenge to develop something new. Challenges are part and parcel of manifestation. Instead of fighting them, let them guide the creative process.

A distinction needs to be drawn between what constitutes manifestation vs. fantasy. It's common for lower-level travelers to try to manifest things beyond their scope. But what constitutes scope? Isn't the whole idea behind manifestation to break free from limiting beliefs and call in a future that is greater than where you are now?

To some degree, manifestation is about stretching your truths by letting go of existing ones. But there are limits. You cannot manifest beyond what you're able to hold. Otherwise, it becomes something you can imagine but not retain. This is what you might call fantasy. If you look closely, you can tell that fantasy causes your mind to lose balance. Fantasy feels chaotic, unruly, and overly fantastic. Your heart is overcome with yearning, a sense of lack about where you are right now, and fear of not getting there, none of which makes for a reliable foundation from which to take action.

Fantasy is when your desires exceed or distort the capacity of your energy self. It introduces more noise and confusion than focus and direction. It's an ecstatic distortion of your Subjective Reality. Ultimately, fantasy is a useless artifact of too much mind. It's a specific way of getting lost in thought.

The field of quantum physics shows how your expectations influence the outcome. In spiritual settings, this is known as intention setting. But if you can't hold the frequency of an intention long enough, there is no consistent call for the particles to assemble themselves accordingly. Instead, your mind sends out confused and chaotic signals. Even the incredible Universe doesn't know what to do with that.

In order to generate and hold a consistent vibration, everything you've learned about on your journey of self-discovery comes into play. Meditation, acceptance, presence, flow, etc. As such, manifestation is not a separate activity you engage in whenever you want something special to happen, particularly something that seems beyond your reach. That's lower-level thinking, where you feel separate from life and wish someone would save you from yourself. True manifestation is always happening, always on. You exude it with every heartbeat, every breath you take. At every moment of your existence, you create your reality based on who you currently are and what you believe to be possible. The less you believe, the more you think is possible, and the better you can manifest. The best manifesters are those who are most self-aware.

It goes without saying that being a master manifester does not translate into flippant, selfish, or reckless behavior. Remember, when you're in the flow, you co-create directly with Source. You're not randomly coming up with ideas. You're a vessel through which life can express itself. In this place of co-creation, there is only divine will. There is only the unknown becoming known. There is only you and pure Source energy turning the formless into form.

Lesson 4
FREEDOM

Level 4 is no longer about healing and figuring yourself out. It's no longer about trying to make sense of the unknowable. It's about shining your light, making an impact on the world, flowing with the greater current, and becoming completely free.

Free from the weight of your beliefs. Free from avoiding your feelings. Free from having to get somewhere. Free from judging everything you encounter. Free from needing to know. Free from seeing what you want to see. Free from resisting what you don't want to see. Free from wanting things. Free from not wanting things. Free from clinging to feelings. Free from loving conditionally. Free from wanting others to be different. Free to be who you are. Free to let your life unfold in ways you could never imagine. Free to enjoy your path's twists and turns. Free from the illusion of predictability. Free to spend more time in Pure Presence. Free to be in receiving mode and open to all possibilities. Free to lose yourself in the endless details of the material world. Free to connect with other humans you would otherwise miss while rushing from A to B. Free to hear your inner voice and follow your body's wisdom. Free to hold space for others to have the experience they need for their evolution. Free to expect the unexpected. Free to recognize the miracle of it all. And – everyone's favorite - free to call in infinite abundance from the ever-expanding Universe. When you no longer want what you want - but want what life wants for you - you experience true freedom.

It's ironic that at lower levels, you spend your whole life pursuing your plan to become free, not realizing your plan keeps you from being free. All the things you think are possible are actually your limitations. Your entire control grid keeps you attached to that which you know and judge.

In other words, everything you do to get somewhere is holding you back from getting there.

Starting with Level 4, all of this complexity falls away. Objective Reality is the name of the game. You no longer yearn for the good old days. You no longer yearn for anything. You experience every situation with a refreshing newness, recognizing its evolving nature. You rarely step outside Pure Presence to see how far you've come. Instead, you flow with a powerful sense of immediate, current, and focused aliveness. You are in total sync with what's happening. The farthest you ever veer is a moment of curiosity about what comes next.

Level 4 is beyond letting go of control. You might even describe it as being out of control - in the best possible way. That is what it means to accept, let go, and flow. Your mind may still try to know things, assign a fixed size, and put life in a box. But at this stage, you're too aware of your thoughts to give away your power like that.

Of course, life continues to bring you growth opportunities. Bigger and more complex situations present themselves to test how much you're prepared to trust and surrender. Time and again, right when you think you've reached your peak, life's unlimited creativity finds a way to push your buttons and show you there's still more room to grow. Level 4 prompts and prods you to become as free and unlimited as life itself.

Lesson 5
TIMELESSNESS

At Level 4, you learn that you're a timeless being. That's not just lofty spiritual chatter. You can actually experience yourself as that. After all, when you flow with the continuous arising and passing of life, you have no conceivable beginning or end. You continue to exist through everything that happens and – more intriguingly – that doesn't happen. You flow with everything that doesn't happen, too.

To fully inhabit your timeless nature, you cannot react to time even in the slightest. Your reactivity gives rise to the experience of time and grants it power over you.

In daily life, not reacting to time looks like this: If you're late to work because you're stuck in traffic, you're just sitting in your car. If you're standing in line at the supermarket, you're just standing where you are. If your alarm clock says 2 am and you have to get up early, you don't see it as being late and worry you'll be tired the next day. You just see it's 2 am. In other words, your ability to stay Peak present is so strong that time no longer elicits a reaction beyond the sheer noticing of it as a practical means of marking temporal change. Nothing more and nothing less.

As long as time is more than just a means to track change - you are not free. You are a slave to the ticking clock. It constantly interferes with Level 4 flow. But when you can absolve yourself from the context of time, then time fades into the background and becomes a non-issue. Time-keeping is still there for practical purposes, but you no longer feel it. There's no urgency to be anywhere because you are where you are. You're not chasing anything because you enjoy being here, not there. You no longer resist change because life is change, and you are life. You no longer fear missing out because where you are is where it's at. You no longer fear death because death doesn't exist in timelessness. There is only leaving your body, but the essence of you stays intact. You might even look forward to the next reincarnation because the current version is getting old. It's good to perform a reboot from time to time. You need a fresh burst of physical energy to continue your journey into even higher levels of awareness.

Lower-level travelers might hypothesize that without the urgency of time, you feel less driven to get anything done.

Rest assured, this is not the case. The Universe has a lot going on that it needs your help with. Remember, this is Level 4. The bigger the vessel you are, the more life wants to express itself through you. The more timeless you are, the more creative you are and the more productive you get. In full flow, you receive downloads faster than you can execute.

As your sense of timelessness grows, cultural events like birthdays and holidays carry much less meaning. Your day-to-day frequency is so high that singling out any particular day to celebrate no longer resonates. While it's important not to reject or diminish the importance put on those occasions by the rest of society, it becomes increasingly important to surround yourself with individuals who equally honor their timeless nature.

To be timeless is to be in complete harmony with every moment. You know no other way than being content because being is contentment. You celebrate everything that *is* because everything that *is* deserves to be celebrated. You experience beauty without clinging to it. You desire wealth without feeling lack. You celebrate others without comparing yourself. You can want more without thinking you're less. You no longer create stories because all there is are moments that string themselves together on their own. You honor your body and treat it like the temple that it is.

LEVEL 4 | Reflections

Level 4 is a time to enjoy the fruits of your labor. You have stepped into the power of your inner truth. In a way, it's like starting all over again, but without the baggage and hindrances that have defined your existence thus far.

REBIRTH

Going from Level 3 to Level 4 is not a transition. It's a rebirth often described as *the phoenix rising from the ashes*. The Phoenix is a legendary golden bird from ancient Greek mythology that can regenerate from its own ashes. It represents the experience of emerging from a catastrophe as a stronger, wiser, more robust person. Level 3's *Dark Night of the Soul* is just that. It burns you to the ground. All your attachments to the world around you are severed, and everything you hold to be true dissolves as you plummet into meaninglessness.

Once you emerge from the darkness, you've been cleansed from the lower frequencies and are ready to inhabit clean Level 4 awareness. There are no energetic holdovers from before. The life you previously built around your conditioned self is no more. While you still honor who you once were, Level 4 is a total transformation. No doubts remain about taking the spiritual path. You have done the work and gone to hell and back. You're ready to redefine your relationship with the world and re-envision a life free of attachment, judgment, and external dictates or preconceived truths. The time has come to live by your greatest awareness.

But with great awareness also comes great change. As you rebuild your life from the ground up, you must put utmost importance on who you surround yourself with and ensure your environment supports and nurtures your highest vibration. Mediocrity is not worth your attention. No job or relationship is worth compromising your inner peace for. That also applies to how you treat yourself. Not a single word you utter can be low-vibe. If it does, you immediately feel it dimming your connection to Source.

At first, it can be daunting to protect your energy from people who live in their heads. Sometimes, these people are your very own family. Generations of engrained patterns and limiting beliefs can bring you down quickly. Before you know it, your sense of gratitude and generosity fades. Your language becomes harsh. You're no longer able to empathize in the same way as before. The noise in your head returns. You feel disoriented and lose your connection to your higher calling. You no longer act based on what's best for all but what's best for you. You struggle to speak up, be true to yourself, and honor your conscience.

As you climb up the awareness ladder, overcoming lower energy fields is one of the ongoing obstacles. The best thing you can do is keep re-arranging the physical world around you to match your wavelength. You can't win if you constantly have to justify your actions, lifestyle, and priorities. It may seem unfair that you have to carve out a new life while the old crowd remains. But when you're no longer willing to perpetuate your suffering, you don't have a choice.

Creating a high-vibe life isn't so straightforward, either. On the one hand, you've never felt this free. But you've also never felt this uncertain. The future is wide open, which is both thrilling and scary. Non-judgment feels light and easy, but it's also unstable and unstructured. Experiencing new, unfamiliar people, places, and things can be stressful in and of itself. But every time you visit your family, friends, and former co-workers, they remind you that you can't go back to your old life. You've seen too much, connected too deeply, been present for too long, and experienced too much peace to revert to how things were. Now, it's all about moving forward, re-arranging the pieces of your life, or letting them go outright. You're committed to doing what it takes to stay in the flow.

That's why you rarely encounter Level 4 travelers in places where low levels of awareness rule. Environments dominated by groupthink, censorship, or limited individual expression are suffocating. You might dip in and out to leave behind some breadcrumbs for others to follow. But you no longer participate in the noisy excesses of pre-Level 4 life. You much prefer simplicity, minimalism, temperance, and stillness over material prestige, entertainment, and career ladders. And that's best done away from the madness of the emotionally abusive, physically harmful, and spiritually vacuous Level 1 world.

It seems unfortunate that in Level 1 societies, the wisest members become ostracized, marginalized, and ridiculed for their inner truth orientation. It seems unjust that those who are connected to greater love are the ones who are relegated to the fringes, while those who live in misalignment and mental chaos continue to rule the roost. But remember, there was a time when you were one of them - in this lifetime or another. There's never, ever any reason to judge anyone, yourself included. Everyone is on their path. It's just that the average frequency across the planet is lower than that of individuals who have dedicated themselves to self-improvement. The best thing you can do is see things for what they are, surround yourself with like-minded, and keep moving forward.

MIRACLES

Level 4 is also the level of miracles. At lower levels of awareness, unusually fortunate events that cannot be explained by rational logic are called miracles. The mind is such a brilliant control freak that it labels the inexplicable as an exception, thereby protecting your existing truth structure while still giving the exception a home on your control grid.

Level 4 does away with all this complexity. All the things you used to create from lack, you now create with full awareness and no expectations. *No expectations* means not assigning meaning. And when you no longer assign meaning, all that remains is the intrinsic miracle that anything exists.

Being in continuous flow means being continuously connected to the miracle. No matter how intense or uncomfortable any situation might become, and conversely, no matter how mundane any given moment might be, a part of you is always aware that the fact this is happening is amazing. And that you can manifest into this amazingness is mind-blowing.

ALONENESS

At Level 4, you're no longer afraid of being alone. Instead, you love spending time with yourself. You no longer need the world to make you feel a certain way because you no longer feel like anything is missing. You've become contained, self-generating, and self-providing. You can still pursue goals or be in relationships, but it becomes a choice. You no longer feel compelled to seek yourself in others because you think you need them for your happiness.

Because that's what you've been doing up until now. You've been putting everything you feel you're missing onto others, be it romance or otherwise, in the form of conditions. And that's fine. Those are invaluable healing relationships where you trigger each other so your wounds become exposed and get addressed. But the pressure comes off when you no longer need someone to be a certain way. The dynamic shifts to where love is free to show up in the most beautiful, empowered way without any expectations putting constraints on it. You can live an exceptional life marked by uninhibited acceptance of yourself and the world around you – whether you're alone or not.

PURPOSE

When you're in the flow, you pull directly from Source. As such, anything you co-create is exclusively for the greater good. Actions you take are no longer focused on personal gain but on promoting the unbridled expression of the divine love for creation. That means with Level 4 awareness, you cannot help but live in service of what's best for all. After doing so much work to release your own blockages, your energy field shifts from an inward orientation to opening up and becoming a healing force for others. You become aware of the unresolved wounds of your ancestors, peers, and other social groups.

Taking on other people's stuff can be irritating at first. *I've done enough work, and now I have to heal others??* It's like you can't catch a break. But endless expansion is part of being a timeliness being. As long as you are in your body, you cannot become stagnant. Life always finds a way to make you grow. The world is never done, so your work is never done. You are now a beacon of greater awareness. You can't hide your light. With personal growth comes a responsibility to share your frequency with the world.

At Level 4, you realize being of service is your ultimate purpose. It has always been in the making. It's the challenges you overcome that you are now an expert at overcoming. It's your darkest moments that turn into your brightest light. It's your struggles that make you resilient. It's your limited beliefs that teach you how to think big. It's your insecurities that turn into the courage to stand for your truth and show others how to do the same. Your hardships shape you into a person of substance and authority, someone who has the authenticity and insight to give back and be a pillar of strength. You've gone from survivor to thriver. From victim to victor. From lost to found.

IMAGINATION

At lower levels of awareness, you think only what you can perceive with your five senses is real, and anything in your imagination is not. Now, at Level 4, you have the personal depth and mental clarity to reflect and realize that your anxiety about the future is also just your imagination. You're imagining what *might* happen. And it's so palpable that it's stressing you out and making you sick. So, how is imagination not real? Why is imagining negative outcomes considered real and visualizing positive ones not? Clearly, there is an unhealthy bias here.

Your body, for one, doesn't know the difference. Look up research on mock surgeries or the placebo effect. The body makes no distinction between an imagined event and one happening right in front of you. Thus, anything you can be present with is real. That includes everything you can imagine since you're imagining it presently. Read that again.

LEVEL 4 | Paradoxes

Level 4 paradoxes exist in a league of their own. They capture the biggest themes and have the power to shift your life to an entirely new vibrational level. But remember, with great power comes great responsibility.

PARADOX #1

The less you believe, the more you understand.

While somewhat of a play on words, the underlying meaning of this paradox is profound. All beliefs are limiting beliefs. All *knowing* is an illusion of permanence that robs you and that which you define of aliveness. When you let go of beliefs and no longer pretend to know, a deeper understanding arises that is beyond the mind. Your intuition comes to life. You sense there is so much more to life than meets the eye. You feel that everything will be alright, no matter what may happen. Your trust in the Universe becomes unshakable – a far cry from the always-anxious, always-comparing state of living in your head. You accept that the only way to live a healthy, happy, inspired life is to let go and go with the flow.

Letting go of knowledge doesn't mean discrediting your expertise. It just means you're no longer attached to a lop-sided reliance on professional priesthood. It means you can maintain a connection to and reverence for the unknown, the mystical, and the magic while still applying your skills and logical reasoning. Zen Buddhism refers to this as a beginner's mind, meaning that a beginner sees endless possibilities and is open to discovery and new solutions, whereas the expert is limited by their beliefs and sees very few options. The key is to recognize that knowledge slows you down. It limits your expansion. You have a much deeper experience of life when you don't feel compelled to compare what happens to what you already know.

PARADOX #2

You gain by giving.

To give without expecting anything in return is the highest form of living. But it can only happen when your own cup is overflowing. This requires you to work through your issues first. You can't heal others before you heal yourself. You can't free others unless you free yourself first. As long as you're still subsumed by attachments and limiting beliefs, every act of giving comes with some degree of conditions and expectations. Because in the early stages of your awareness journey, all of your behavior is conditional. When you enter Level 4, your expectations disappear, no longer diluting your efforts and choices.

Again, the fruits of your labor always reflect the motivation that drives them. If you give from lack, people-pleasing, or need for control, the outcome will perpetuate the energy of the volition you acted from. To yield pure results, you must give purely. To give purely, you must purify yourself first.

PARADOX #3

You find yourself when you stop trying to find yourself.

At this point in your journey of self-realization, you've taken classes, talks, workshops, retreats, and other healing activities and events. You've spent hours absorbing podcasts, webinars, blogs, and books, looking for answers to your most pressing questions. You have a list of your favorite yoga instructors, meditation teachers, and spiritual speakers. You've replaced your old circle of friends with a new tribe of like-minded seekers who embrace working on themselves.

From dissolving traumas to building self-worth to releasing limiting beliefs and practicing self-love, everyone is trying to heal, trying to surrender, and trying to become more enlightened. And that's the blocker: they're trying.

Stop trying. Trying is not your natural state. Birds don't try to fly. Flowers don't try to bloom. Trying contains so much resistance. As long as you seek, you haven't arrived. As long as you want it, it cannot materialize. As long as you hold the thought of not yet being who you want to be, you can't be that person. *Trying* not only gets in the way of you getting there, it makes you miserable in the meantime. The more you long to reach a goal, the more your longing blocks you from reaching it. Read that again.

PARADOX #4

To get what you want, you must not want it.

This is one of the hardest paradoxes to implement. How do you feel motivated if not by want? How do you move forward without resisting where you are? How do you manifest change without reinforcing lack?

If you've ever had an overly needy person come to you, you'll know how instantly repulsive their energy is. It's an obvious example of how energy works. When you really want something, you push away receiving it. The same principle applies to everything else in life. You get love not by wanting it from others but by cultivating it within yourself. You get abundance when you already feel like you have everything you need. Life comes to you when you don't need it to look a certain way. Energy flows in the absence of conditions.

You may notice the irony in that. What good is it to receive those things after you already feel like you have them? But that's exactly the point. How you feel is not dependent on your environment. It's dependent on you. Nothing stands in the way of you living your best life possible other than yourself. You don't need circumstances to be a certain way. You don't need anyone else. You just need yourself. Everything you want is already inside of you.

Recognize how sensitive energy is. You cannot fool it. You cannot bypass it. You cannot go about things half-heartedly. What you put in is what you get out. You must be fine-tuned to the highest, purest degree if you want peace, flow, and bliss. Then, what you want comes to you without even trying.

PARADOX #5

As long as you keep looking, you remain lost.

Looking for the path reinforces feeling lost. If you keep looking forever, you will stay lost forever. There must come a point when you stop looking.

That point comes when you cultivate Pure Presence. It's impossible to feel lost if right now is all you're giving your attention to. It's impossible to be anxious when you're present because anxiety is always about the future. It's impossible to feel incomplete right now because in Pure Presence, the mind isn't involved, so you can't compare yourself to anything. Therefore, right now, you're always complete.

Becoming a seeker and looking for a better way is part of your evolution. That's what your suffering prompts you to do. Eventually, however, you get tired of feeling lost and realize it's also a part of your journey to let go of the *seeker* label. That's when you learn to settle into the absence of any identity. To become truly free, you must become nothing.

LEVEL 4 | Summary

Once you get to Level 4, your life will never be the same. And that's a beautiful, fundamental truth. It's at the heart of your expanding awareness. Accepting that no two moments are alike frees you from your attachments and gives you the trust and resilience to keep growing.

Of course, it's hard when the people closest to you are the most unaware. But don't despair. With time, your energy field becomes more sturdy and self-contained. Lower frequencies bounce right off you or go straight through you. Level 4 teaches you how to become an energy master. You learn that energy knows no boundaries and has no limits. By embracing your limitless nature, you are now free to flow.

Your primary Level 4 task is learning how flow is created and maintained and organizing your life around it. The cleaner and uninterrupted your frequency, the greater the flow, and the more powerful and focused your manifestation powers become. This includes creating a life of freedom like nothing you could have imagined. Once you're free, you can help others do the same.

At this point, you're no longer putting foundational pillars in place. You worked that out during Levels 1-3. Now, it's about how to build a new life on top of them. All the seemingly disparate pieces of yourself have come together to give shape to your true power, peace, and purpose. And with that, your life shifts into a higher gear you didn't know existed. Finally, you've arrived.

Here are the main behaviors to check off and reflect on. You're ready to graduate from Level 4 when:

☐ You spend most of your time in flow. It's very obvious when you're not in it.

☐ You've redesigned your life from the ground up. Where, how, and with whom is now in alignment.

☐ You're a powerful manifester. Nothing holds you back. You have no limiting beliefs about what's possible.

☐ Freedom is your highest currency.

☐ You're never stressed. Time does not exist other than for practical matters.

☐ You expect the unexpected. You trust your co-creator, so miracles are normal.

☐ You enjoy extended periods of quiet time alone.

☐ Your imagination is one of your superpowers.

☐ You hear your intuition loud and clear. Life speaks to you.

- You prefer not knowing. The less you know, the more is possible.

- You can observe your thoughts without reacting to them.

- You can feel your feelings fully without reacting to them.

- You are consistent and uncompromising in your meditation practice and self-care routine.

- You see everyday situations as opportunities to practice Pure Presence.

- You know you can only give when you've taken care of your needs first.

- You understand that life is a blank slate, and it's your choice to assign meaning.

- You can feel that *trying* is not a natural state.

- You understand all wanting comes from lack and reinforces not having.

- You no longer want what you want. You want what life wants for you.

- You love yourself, and you love life.

LEVEL 4 | Next Steps

You can see that graduating from Level 4 is not for slackers. Even when you've perfected flow and feel infinitely powerful, it doesn't mean you can thumb your nose at the system. You cannot go off-roading or do your own thing. You must continue to play by the rules. There is so much to work on. Cultivating an even higher frequency now requires surgical precision. There's no punching the clock or showing up half-hearted.

After all, your journey has primed you to co-create with Source. Talk about a high-profile partner. Conscious creation is the greatest contribution you can make to the planet. You must stay vigilant and consistent within yourself and stand firm against the lower ends of the energy spectrum. Here are some steps to help you fully inhabit your Level 4 powers:

1. Maintain flow. You cannot do it all alone. You must generate and maintain flow and let yourself be carried by the greater current. To do so, firmly establish yourself in all the basic principles of flow: Downstream vs upstream. Forward vs backward. Momentum vs stagnation. Allowing vs. pushing. These orientations must be the primary components of your life. Every choice and decision should abide by these principles. You know you're there when it feels like you're moving mountains with ease and things are falling into place on their own.

2. Optimize your body, mind, and spirit. Treat yourself as the vessel of conscious creation that you are. Steer clear of lifestyle choices and habits that numb your vibration. Poor sleep numbs you. Junk food numbs you. Taking in violent material numbs you. Drugs and anti-depressants numb you. Watching the news, video games, and endlessly scrolling through social media numbs you. Level 4 demands that you align only with behaviors that serve your well-being and eliminate those that don't. Again, everything you create contains you.

3. Become that which you want to manifest. If you want to manifest abundance, you need to feel abundant first. If you want to manifest an amazing partner, become amazing first. You attract that which you are. That's why it's so hard to manifest at lower levels of awareness. The things you desire are typically motivated by lack, not feeling good enough, or avoiding your traumas and fears. But when you create from Level 4 flow, your volition is pure. So, what you manifest is, too.

This is where you can use your mind's tendency to compare

itself: Write down the qualities you admire in someone you look up to or list the qualities you look for in a potential life mate. Then, turn that list around, put your name on it, and start working on those qualities within yourself. Subconsciously, you seek to complete yourself through others. Use this exercise as a means to guide you in your self-reflection journey.

4. Stay in creation mode. Life constantly cycles through three modes: creation, maintenance, and destruction. As always, the outcome depends on your source motivation. When you create from passion, you can let it go once it's complete and move on to the next thing. You stay in creation mode and keep re-inventing yourself. But when you create from lack or fear, you cling to what you've created because it represents the bandage for your wound. You quickly fall into steering and controlling. Eventually, destruction rolls in because it's unnatural to be standing still. Either the conditions around you change, or you get bored and make changes yourself. So, keep creating. Stay in sync with your evolution. That way, maintenance and destruction never catch up to you.

5. Set achievable goals. While it's good to have a big vision, when it comes to the practical, the secret to manifesting effectively is to pick achievable goals. If your goal is too far in the future or it's too big and complex, your tractor beam gets too thin to pull it into your experience. On the level of quantum physics, the area you are focused on attracting is either too big or too far away to motivate matter to assemble according to your vision. So, the power of your intention must match what you can effectively feel as real. But if it takes too long for traction to build and only parts of your vision to materialize, you'll either lose focus or exit your body before you see any tangible results. Remember, manifestation isn't some blind belief. It's what you can genuinely see happening.

6. Avoid any notions of how and when. Any ideas you harbor about how something needs to happen restrict your energy field and block matter from rearranging most expediently. The moment you think it should happen one war or another, it interferes with the natural manifestation process. Similarly, expectations of *when* you can see results are also detrimental. When you start looking for proof, you get impatient, lose the balance of your mind, and your expectations take you out of the flow. To maximize your creation powers, stay in Pure Presence and accept the feeling of being *here*, not longing to be *there*.

7. Be patient. It's impossible to know the timeline of how things are meant to unfold. There may be parts of you that still need growing and fine-tuning before you are ready for a bigger shift to take place. Or some seemingly unrelated event must happen elsewhere for your breakthrough moment to come together. All you can do is stay in the flow, respond to what shows up, follow your inner voice, and take clear action. This is the path of least resistance and most alertness. This is the most effective way forward. In this setting, patience no longer takes effort. It's simply the way you operate. It is a natural by-product of presence, acceptance, and flow. Typically, you don't notice your patience until someone else comments on it. So, do not despair if patience has not been your strong suit thus far. At Level 4, being patient is much easier than it used to be when you were stuck with all the noise in your head.

8. Receive equally. The ability to receive plays an integral part in keeping the flow going. There always needs to be a balance between giving and receiving. Otherwise, your energy field is too lopsided. If you're uncomfortable receiving, it means there's a limiting belief in your system. It could indicate a lack of self-worth, guilt or shame around abundance, a tendency to be a people-pleaser, etc. Whatever it may be, identify it and work through it. Learn to receive with the same open heart from which you give. Flow means abundance for all.

9. Keep doing breathwork and body scanning. Daily meditation continues to be the most crucial building block of your mindfulness practice. If you fall off the wagon, you get sucked back into mental reactivity and lose your connection to the flow. A firm commitment to a daily meditation practice is a must. Always start with breathwork followed by body scanning. Do as much of each as you feel is appropriate. There may be times when you just feel like doing one or the other. That's ok, too. Increase your practice to twice a day for at least 30-60 minutes each. Mornings and evenings are still best. At this point, you're an expert meditator. There shouldn't be any separation between your meditative state and the rest of your day. You bring peace, presence, and flow wherever you go.

10. Attend silent meditation retreats. The best way to generate greater thought awareness is by sitting in silence for extended periods and observing your thoughts. This is best done at silent meditation retreats that last at least a week. Towards the end of such retreats, your mind becomes so highly sensitive that you can feel the weight of your thoughts. That's when you realize that giving your attention to any thought, whether negative or positive, comes with an energetic weight. Thus, you become more vigilant in your overall thought awareness. Consider doing this deep cleanse for the mind at regular intervals to bolster your regular daily practice. Eventually, the line between meditation and the rest of your life blends, and you always find yourself in a meditative state.

LEVEL 5

"As"

Welcome to Level 5. The final frontier. The theme for this level is "As" because life isn't just flowing through you. It's happening *as* you.

While Level 4 is about no resistance, no attachments, and no limiting beliefs, Level 5 is about no *self*. That's right. All that talk about finding your true self - you can now let go of it again.

In many ways, Level 5 is not a new level of self-awareness. It's more like dissolving any remaining awareness of self into nothingness. You're no longer the container through which life flows because being a container invokes boundaries and a hint of separateness. You're no longer in full acceptance of something that's happened because acceptance implies that you and the happening are distinct energy fields. You no longer think that everything is possible because doing so implies something not being possible. Level 5 teaches you these are still just concepts that only exist in your mind. And while they have been helpful and necessary crutches in getting you here, they are mental artifacts that limit the true totality of your being, which is to be one with life.

Level 5 lessons help you identify the last remaining constraints that keep your sense of *me* intact. These lessons take you to the outer boundaries of how you experience yourself and challenge you to dissolve them. Because that's what this whole journey is about: Total dissolution of self. Total immersion in the unknown and unknowable. It's about bringing perfect divine order to the universe by becoming one with all there is.

When you experience oneness - or *unity consciousness* - you are not just connected to the moment of unfolding. You are one with it. You *are* it. You're no longer a co-creator transforming the immaterial into material. You're the creation. You're everything that emerges. You're all there is.

There may not be much suffering at Level 5, but the lessons are no less monumental. Oneness demands absolute purity. Here are the Level 5 lessons that take you there.

LEVEL 5 | Lessons

Lesson 1
META-AWARENESS

By now, you can see the tremendous evolution of your awareness.

At Level 1, being aware simply means paying attention to your environment. For example, you're aware of pedestrians crossing the street up ahead. Or you're aware it's raining, and you should take an umbrella before leaving the house. You can also be aware of danger or a threat. This type of situational awareness is very basic and closely tied to your knowledge. What you know is what you're aware of.

Level 2 makes you more aware of the connection between yourself and your environment and that you ultimately create your reality. Relinquishing control and taking responsibility for your happiness requires tremendous personal growth and fosters deep insight into your impact on the world.

The lid comes off at Level 3, where it's all about accepting yourself and your circumstances, understanding the impermanent nature of life, and cultivating deep awareness around your motives, such as when you create from lack.

Finally, at Level 4, your awareness reaches new heights as you enjoy Pure Presence, flow downstream, and manifest with the greater current. With Subjective Reality no longer clouding your mind, you can see things as they are. And when you consistently see things as they are, something extraordinary happens: You notice yourself observing things. In other words, a witness is witnessing the witness. In other words, you're aware of being aware. Welcome to Level 5 *Meta-Awareness*.

The term *meta* comes from Greek and means *beyond* the usual scope. Prior to Level 5, the scope of your awareness is limited to your body, your person, your situation, and your environment. Your awareness flows to and from *you*.

But in Meta-Awareness, your awareness expands to include itself, thereby transcending your body and concept of *me*. You now experience life from a place outside of your physical being. It's a comprehensive perspective on anything and everything, free of the dynamics and constraints of your human identity. Your awareness is now so detached from the material dimension that your existence carries no greater value than your non-existence. In other words, you are no longer bound to form. Instead, you're completely free to be nothing, which is when you become available to be everything.

With Meta-Awareness, you finally become aware of your spiritual essence. You see straight through the material world and its machinations. You can use your frequency to impact anything from anywhere. You can instantly transport your energetic self to where you feel called to explore, regardless of distance or dimension. You can connect with any version of reality that arises in the unfolding and be the space around it.

Curiously, you've experienced Meta-Awareness before without even realizing it.

Remember how, at lower levels, your mind keeps drifting, and you catch yourself being lost in thought? Without realizing it, it's Meta-Awareness that snaps you out of it and brings you back to Pure Presence. Regular awareness cannot do this because it is tied to your senses and can't transcend what you're sensing.

But Meta-Awareness can. It does so essentially by acting as a capacitor - a component that stores and releases electrical energy - for holding the friction that builds up when you're absent-minded and out of sync with life. As the capacitor fills up, the pressure accrues until it finally results in a powerful discharge. A burst of energy ripples through your mind and body, dispelling the heavy and erratic thought patterns from being lost in thought and pulling you back into Pure Presence.

But only for a moment. For a few seconds, you are aware of having been unaware. From there, you're likely to get lost in thought again, and the whole thing repeats. At Level 3 and below, you spend up to two-thirds of your day in this cycle.

You can try it out for yourself. The next time you come out of a mental rabbit hole, pay close attention. Notice how, for a short time after snapping back, you experience Level 5 Meta-Awareness. In that brief moment, you are completely clear, still, and thoughtless.

Level 5 is about learning to be meta-aware all the time so you can access the field of oneness. But this is a highly refined operation. To consistently see things as they are entails letting go of all labels and definitions, anything and everything that generates even a hint of subjectivity. That includes everything you ever experienced yourself to be. All the memories, emotions, and events. All the judgments of *good and bad* or *right and wrong*. The entire personal narrative of who you once were, who you are now, and where you're going. Any reaction to time or sense of beginnings and endings. You even have to let go of everything you manifest at Level 4. You can't see clearly until there is nothing left of you.

Until now, everything you ever believed about yourself limited you to only those beliefs. Your control grid has enforced a narrow focus your entire life. By believing you are a few things, you've kept yourself from being everything else, perpetuating separateness from the world around you. Even at Level 4, flow is a way to move *through* everything. But you're still not everything.

Ultimately, it's really simple. Unity consciousness is right there in front of you, accessible to all who have made the journey of letting go of who they're not. You are not your thoughts, not your feelings, and certainly not what others think of you. You are not your age, name, job title, or the person who owns this or that. You are not your interpretation of anything that's ever happened or any other element in your Subjective Reality. You are not your body, brain, or personality. And above all, you are not your mind.

If all this is over your head, don't worry. Forget the theory. Just enjoy the process. At Level 5, there is so much to enjoy. The state of Meta-Awareness isn't just an endless ocean of calm. It also contains a sense of infinity, omniscience, and—curiously—a cosmic sense of humor about how silly, flawed, and fantastically bizarre the entire human experience is. You cannot help but chuckle at seeing humans obsess over their own triviality.

Lesson 2
STILLNESS

The next essential requirement for oneness is *stillness.*

At Levels 1 through 3, you perceive the world as harsh, loud, ugly, and aggressive. It feels like everyone is out to get you, resources are limited, and you must look for your advantage in every situation. Your mind is fearful and always on the lookout for danger and threat. You even turn on yourself in the form of a fierce inner critic. In more ways than one, you are your own worst enemy.

Level 4 takes you in the opposite direction. Everything quiets down. Your nervous system cools off. You enjoy *me* time and look forward to solitude. Loneliness is no longer a threat.

You are no longer in any rush to get anywhere because where you are is where everything is. Nothing deserves to be rejected or discredited. Everything is equally valid and has its purpose. That's how you access the state of flow.

But at Level 5, Meta-Awareness grants you access to another realm altogether. It is not the usual stillness you might associate with quieting your mind, sitting in silence, or being comfortable alone. In fact, it doesn't come from you at all. This stillness is an all-pervasive, crystal-clear energy emanating deep from within the fabric of the Universe. It is the space in which everything material and immaterial exists. Everything that takes form is a temporary material expression that arises from this stillness and eventually subsides back into it. It's like the Buddha Board of Life, where things manifest before being wiped away by the winds of change.

If you pay close attention, you can sense this stillness, primarily by deduction. It's what remains when you take away everything that exists. The earth, the stars, the galaxy, all neighboring galaxies. Keep removing objects from your Meta-Awareness until nothing is left. And then you see it. There is something that everything is created into or onto. That is stillness. It's the canvas upon which life paints itself.

Stillness is what you previously experienced as the *unknown* – because it contained fear and uncertainty. Once you dissolve the fear, the unknown turns into stillness. This stillness is the outer boundary of the world of form. It is not consciousness itself, which cannot be sensed, as any sensing would itself be consciousness. But it's as close as you can get from within the material dimension using your human capabilities.

When you tune into this stillness, you experience an expansive state of infinite spaciousness, peaceful meaninglessness, and all-knowingness. This gives rise to a divine reassurance that everything is perfect because it *is,* and nothing is important enough to get upset about when it *isn't.* All answers arise from this stillness, which is where all creation takes place.

You don't have to do anything to achieve Level 5 stillness. In fact, you have to do nothing. You have to believe nothing. You have to cling to nothing. You have to be nothing. In the absence of being anything, you become one with everything.

Maintaining your meta-aware state and connection to stillness takes energy. More than ever, proper rest, nutrition, and clean living are essential to maintain the awareness powerhouse that you have become. As long as you stay still, the world cannot get to you because you are the world. You cannot lose because everything created is automatically a win. You cannot get lost because you're always on the path of everywhere and nowhere. You're not afraid of yourself because there is no self. You don't need answers because there are no questions. Everything is going your way because you're going the way of everything.

Lesson 3
SURRENDER

By now, you've learned that *acceptance* is the one quality that consistently moves you up the awareness ladder. Acceptance lets you meet what is, where it is, when it is, and how it is. It empowers you to experience Objective Reality.

But there is an even deeper aspect to acceptance that takes you beyond the reality of the present moment. And that is *surrender*.

When you surrender, you give yourself over to what you can't see, what hasn't materialized yet, and that you can't tune into because it arises from places that can't be perceived, from what is in store for you cosmically.

You may have karmic debt that you need to repay. Corrective measures at the micro-energetic level may need to happen. You may need to heal in ways you could never observe or comprehend. There are elements at play that reach into your earthly life from other dimensions - guides and angels and even the hand of God - all of whom want to help move you forward - if only you let them. And the best way to let them do their work is to surrender. Life is hard enough as it is. Why go it alone? If you want true peace, if you want the full experience, you have no choice but to surrender to what you don't know. And you don't know what you don't know. You barely remember anything from the past year, let alone past lifetimes. Surrender is needed because you've stopped predicting the future long ago, and you can't read God's mind.

Ironically, by surrendering, you gain all the things you are afraid of losing by surrendering. Trust, confidence, self-love, peace, clarity, freedom, connection to a higher power, and abundance. Obviously, there is no greater abundance than being one with all there is.

The deeper your surrender, the deeper you connect to stillness. You could even say you surrender *to* stillness. But it doesn't end there. Once you truly surrender, you can finally just *be*.

Lesson 4
BEING

Being is the state of total surrender. It's a comprehensive letting go of everything, including many of the crutches that have gotten you here. Control, doubts, fears, reactivity, the past, the future, attachment to outcome and yourself – not a hint of it can remain. Even the slightest trace takes you out of Meta-Awareness, cuts you off from stillness, and takes you out of true surrender.

At lower levels, *being* is interpreted as inactivity. But nothing could be more misguided. *Being* arises from continuous flow. It means you're confident, connected, and clued in—not just because you're more efficient, effective, and productive than ever before, not just because you're at peace with your thoughts, feelings, and circumstances, but because you are always one with where you are.

As such, *being* is your most powerful doing. It's like passengers on a train sitting still while the vehicle around them moves on their behalf. When you are always flowing, with no resistance or reactivity to take you out of it, the greater current takes over, and you can sink into being.

Despite its power, *being* is also the most peaceful state. Far from being concerned with outcomes, following outside voices, or manifesting from lack, you can watch the noisy world around you zip by. Far from thinking this is your life to live, you rest in the cradle of total surrender to who you are without a hint of wanting to be someone you're not. And when you let go of who you think you should be, you can finally let yourself be.

Once you let yourself be, you can let all of life be. All judgment evaporates. All resistance falls away. All of *you* disappears. Just consistent, maximum flow. You realize you've defined yourself this whole time through criticism, judgment, and limiting beliefs. All detours and delays stem from there.

It seems so obvious now. Yet, you've traveled the longest, hardest road to reach this point. All your life, everything you've ever struggled with and pushed against, all the problems you identified with and took on as your own, have come from not letting yourself be. *Being* is harmony. Everything else isn't.

Learning just to *be* is the culmination of your journey. It's all you've ever wanted—not the bling, not the glitz, not the house, not the accomplishments, or the perfect family. Deep down, being is what you've yearned for. When you can *be,* it feels like nothing's missing.

At lower levels, meditation helps you find refuge from loneliness and victimhood. Then, you learn to live mindfully in earnest, using meditation as a tool to improve concentration and let solutions come to you, as opposed to thinking you must create them. Eventually, a solid daily practice ensures continued flow and manifestation.

But at Level 5, meditation falls away completely. *Being* is a continuous meditative state where a separate meditation practice is no longer needed because being *is* the meditative state. You engage with every detail of your environment with utmost curiosity, care, and compassion. You treat the world the way you would treat every last fiber of yourself. When you have no resistance, you are pulled into everything. By being nothing, you become one with all.

Lesson 5
LOVE

By reaching Level 5, you have worked through various stages of deep social conditioning, personal issues, and ancestral trauma. You have learned to come out of reactivity, practiced Pure Presence, and expanded into Meta-Awareness. All of these milestones entail tremendous developments in your life. They take you deeper into yourself and make you become a bigger person than you could have ever imagined. You have learned to let go of things you once considered the absolute truth. You have learned to accept things that you once deemed unacceptable. You have learned to make stillness a way of life, recognize your timeless nature, and focus all your being on being. What is left to do after you surrender everything, including your sense of *me?* What else is there to propel you into the state of oneness with all there is? What gives you the final push to actually unify?

All the lessons you've mastered on this long journey have been about no longer getting in the way of the unfolding of life. *Meta-Awareness, stillness, surrender, and being* clear the path to unity consciousness. But there is only one energy in the Universe that pulls you into it. That energy is love.

Love is not a feeling you generate to show affection to yourself or others. Rather, it's the energy that reveals itself as always having been there when you stop criticizing, judging, and hating. It emerges when you leave the labels and definitions of the mind behind. It arises when you detach from everything you think you are. Love is all there is when you stop thinking.

Love is the central energy that inhabits everything in existence. That includes you. Love takes you beyond acceptance. It takes you beyond flow. It even takes you beyond Objective Reality. True love – without conditional or expectations – requires nothing in return because there are no directions in oneness. You don't create love - it's always been there. You don't generate it – you become it. Or rather, you realize you've been it all along. You've just been keeping yourself separate from it.

Level 5 love is the feeling that you're exactly where you're supposed to be. Love is knowing the moment couldn't be more perfect than what it is. The chirping of birds is perfect. The wind howling through window cracks is perfect. The honks during rush hour are perfect. The construction site next door is perfect. Your co-worker who triggers you is perfect. Your neighbor talking endlessly on the phone is perfect. The imperfections of your dog or cat are perfect. Your family is perfect. And you are perfect. This is what it feels like, not just to be *in* the moment but to *be* the moment.

To love something simply because it exists is divine love. To be led by divine love is divine guidance. It is the highest form of intelligence. And it is instant. It doesn't require consideration or proof. The very moment something appears, it already comes in with the highest purpose, that of its sheer existence. In Level 5 oneness, your purpose is to love everything.

Just how pure your love is quickly exposed in romantic relationships. An intimate partner is the ultimate mirror for all your attachments, judgments, expectations, fears, and lack of self-worth. Getting to know each other is like bringing everything you need to work on to the surface in a nanosecond.

One of the great misconceptions of modern dating is that you need to know each other first before committing. But knowing only gives rise to comparison and judgment. It is the basis for finding reasons to push yourselves apart. Sure, you want some basic assurances regarding health and safety. However, a commitment based on a checklist is as unsteady and arbitrary as the expectations and projections behind it.

Knowing takes away all the mystery, all the fun of discovery, and all of the journey. A true love connection doesn't come from analyzing, comparing, or putting conditions on one another. It comes from a soul connection that unites you through each other to a higher power to which you both answer. With that pure love frequency in place, you can enjoy the discovery of what your human forms are like. You are free to explore every facet of each other's personalities without fear of letdown or that unmet conditions might upset your bond.

Again, your bond is not to each other but through each other to a higher power. In the absence of conditions, only unconditional love remains. Two people who don't put any constraints on each other are ready to form a sacred union and embark on a joint mission to bring greater awareness into the world.

That doesn't mean you should hold off on romance until you're perfect. You might wait forever. Just realize until you can let each other be, you are in healing-each-other mode. In a mature relationship, you can share your triggers and work through the wounds that come to the surface. In a more combustible relationship, it likely means crash and burn. Either way, lessons are learned, self-awareness grows, and everyone becomes a deeper, wiser person. Heartache and heartbreak are some of the toughest lessons. But they are also excellent accelerators of your evolution.

This love for everything begins with you. To experience yourself as one, you must learn to love yourself with every fiber. If there's even the slightest hint of not loving who you are, it blocks you from loving others in that same way. To experience the fullness of life, you must be full of love for yourself.

Once you love yourself, you love everything. You see its perfection. Not because you judge it to be perfect, but because seeing the perfection arises out of love. You see the ease with which it all unfolds. You see the deep, infinite desire that wants all that exists to be what it is meant to be. That includes you. The passion for creation you have emerged from, the breathtaking magnitude from which you have arisen, is the paradise to which you return.

To love is a serious commitment. It is to become that which you have worked so hard to learn to witness. Universal love is the meshing that makes you one with all. There still is, of course, your physical presence. You still have a name, a body, and a likeness through which you engage with the material world. You can still enjoy the senses and marvel at the beauty and perfection of it all. You can still have goals and enjoy the pursuit. The big difference is you are enjoying life without needing it to be one way or another. It can just be the way it wants to be. You arise with situations and pass and transform into the next. Big, small, significant, or insignificant, these descriptors no longer apply. To be in love is to be free.

LEVEL 5 | Reflections

Level 5 brings a flurry of insights that are no longer about self but about the nature of life, why anything exists, and the larger forces at play.

YOU'RE NOT A HUMAN BEING

At lower levels of awareness, you blindly identify with your thoughts and feelings about yourself and everything that happens. You think there is a singular reality and that everyone should be like you. You believe that whatever you're focused on is the only thing that matters, and what matters most is what others think. You seek to control your environment to cover up unhealed emotional traumas. You think you are your body, name, and job title. You think you are a husband, father, or the owner of your house. The lowest level of awareness is believing you are human.

But you are not human. You are not your body, gender, name, job title, or any of those other things. You are simply an energy form with varying degrees of awareness. And you're here for the adventure of helping awareness become aware of itself.

The pull from your human self to your spiritual self is intrinsic and ongoing. It may not move as quickly as the modern-day attention span would like it to, but it's always happening. There are endless things to become aware of within yourself and everything around you. Your journey starts with forming attachments to the material world and ends with finding back to your full, spiritual self. Along the way, you acquire knowledge, only to realize what you know is a tiny speck of what's out there, which ultimately awakens you to the vastness of everything you don't know.

Additionally, somewhere in the ether, there is an ever-present awareness potential between you and everything that has yet to be created. Just because something hasn't taken shape doesn't mean it doesn't exist. Evolution builds on what already exists. Thus, there is a certain universal intention you can pick up on, like reading the mind of a close friend or partner whom you've known for a very long time. That's why, in Level 4 flow, there is a sense of familiarity as each new moment arrives, only to dissolve again at Level 5 when you become one with creation. You can see the beautiful ebb and flow of universal intelligence and how it guides you from one station of life to another.

Whether you like geeking out on diverse philosophical perspectives or prefer to just live your life, you cannot help but become more aware. In fact, with every bio-chemical exchange of your skin with the environment and every pulse of your energy field, greater awareness is taking shape. You can't look out the window without adding greater awareness to your being. No matter how incremental, as long as you're alive, you're expanding in every living, breathing moment. Ideas and insights are constantly beaming at you from your surroundings, the galaxies above, and Mother Earth below. Every cell in you is becoming more conscious as it fulfills its purpose.

So, stop resisting your true nature. You're a perpetual awareness generator. Your life happens at the edge where unaware becomes aware, where unreal becomes real, and where formless becomes form. You can fight it or accept it. The choice is yours.

THE ENERGY SPECTRUM

Less aware energy vibrates lower, and more aware energy vibrates higher. But all frequencies exist all the time. The physical dimension comprises a full spectrum of continuous and ever-present energy. As such, less aware energy doesn't somehow dissolve when you become more aware. You just change your tuning. What version of life you get is simply a question of which vibration you're tuned to.

Depending on your tuning, you experience whatever the associated reality is. At the lower end, closer to Subjective Reality, life moves slowly, change is tedious, and your outlook is narrow. Your behavior tends to be blind and repetitive. You encounter dark roads, choices feel heavy, and you only see limited options. Your mind is mired in concepts like past and future. Life is static, and you feel stuck and uninspired.

At the higher end of the spectrum, closer to Objective Reality, you feel light and flowing. There is a constant breeze of new insights and stimulating impulses. Your mind is present with your circumstances and doesn't linger on moments. Life feels dynamic—like an infinity pool—and just keeps flowing. You have no fears or limits and are excited to see what the next moment brings.

The better you know yourself, the better your decisions and the higher your vibration. Eventually, you transcend the physical dimension when you reach the pure state of unity consciousness. This is your natural state, anyway. Only your attachments to the material world and identification with thoughts have weighed you down. But the more you stand in your truth, the more firmly you are anchored on the upper end of the energy spectrum.

All forms of life operate somewhere on the spectrum. This includes all life forms, plants, animals, and even rocks – everything that consists of vibrating molecules, which is everything. What makes humans unique is they have much greater mobility when it comes to adjusting their tuning and, thus, their position on the scale.

While there are periods of accelerated growth in everyone's life, overall, changing your tuning is a long, arduous journey – in large part due to the limitations of the physical body. There's only so much transformation it can handle in each lifetime before it needs to turn over. That's when death happens. It's like a system reboot to clear out memory, free up storage, and pass your last state of consciousness to a fresher body and mind. It's how life stays energized, mixes things up, and ensures nothing gets stuck.

At rebirth, it may take some time to reorient yourself and sift through the barrage of outside influences. Eventually, however, you catch up to where you last left off and continue on your path. The circumstances you're born into add variety, and nature and nurture are always wildcards. But these are small variables in the greater scheme of things. Every situation is an opportunity to experience yourself in different, nuanced ways. The more pronounced the situation, the stronger the mirror effect, and the more accelerated your self-knowing becomes.

ORIGINS OF THE UNIVERSE

Whenever you catch a breath, you might reflect on life's inner workings and wonder about its origins. When did it start? Who or what started it? And why and how? This desire to know has been part of humanity since the dawn of time. Yet, the answer is so simple that it's beyond remarkable that it's eluded even the brightest minds. Keyword *mind*.

First of all, linear time – which you presume when you think of origin – is a mental construct, primarily as memories of the past and projections for the future. This is why time is an illusion. In Pure Presence—the state we cultivate throughout our journey—time ceases to exist. And with it, so do beginnings and endings. And when beginnings and endings vanish, so does the need to know when something started. Once you are anchored in your infinite nature, it's no longer a question of when did the universe start. It's a matter of no longer experiencing reality in terms that make you ask that question. In other words, no longer living in your head.

The only one interested in defining and explaining the origins of the universe – or anything else, for that matter – is the mind. No one else cares. The tree doesn't care. The squirrel doesn't care. The moon doesn't care. You don't even care when you're not in your head.

You need to know very little to be happy, whereas your mind never knows enough, thereby creating lack and misery. Your true nature is to be boundless and infinite, whereas your mind is all about control and limitations. The more you surrender, the less you feel the need to jump through every mental hoop that comes your way. With enough awareness, you can leave questions like *who created this?* aside and focus on the only thing that matters: the reality in front of you that you are co-creating.

Your journey is learning to let go of the obsession with knowing everything, to be at peace without being in control, to take the next step without seeing the path, to be inspired by more than cause and effect, to rewire your brain to embrace the unknown, to create for the sake of creating, and to accept that something can exist without you needing to explain it.

Questions arise from the state of separateness. Once you are one with all that exists, you no longer question its existence. It's as simple as that.

SOCIAL IMPACT

As one reaches the highest levels of awareness, the way one sees and engages with the world dramatically changes. This raises complex questions about how to best organize society so that people at different stations of life can not only coexist but thrive together.

Your level of awareness affects every decision you make in your life, from education to career path to medicine to lifestyle and relationships. Everything is directly related to how aware you are. Furthermore, your awareness is ever-evolving. Continued growth is the whole point of your existence. Therefore, there must be enough breathing room and flexibility in social and legal frameworks to allow for maximum personal learning and expansion. The more a society insists on a singular version of life, the more stifled and muted every individual's journey of self-discovery gets. A society that limits the pathways an individual can take – often under the premise of protecting the whole – winds up undermining the mental health and spiritual well-being of the entire population.

Typically, the more aware you are, the more you experience large, rigid organizations as soul-sucking and spirit-crushing. Similarly, an overly planned and structured society stifles individuals from working their way up the awareness ladder and discourages them from making choices in alignment with their inner truth. It's much easier to govern blind rule followers, which is what you are at Level 1. For those who have invested in their personal development, it gets increasingly difficult to stay true to your spiritual essence when your environment thinks that going to a meditation retreat means you've joined a cult.

In contrast, a society that values spiritual growth accommodates different lifestyles, communities, and various information sources. Freedom of speech and self-expression are paramount. In fact, freedom of speech is the great equalizer between different levels of awareness. There must be a town square where all truths can be seen and heard. Feeling seen and heard is a big part of what moves people from one level of awareness to the next.

Freedom of self-expression does not mean lawlessness and chaos. It doesn't mean that being more or less aware exempts you from the social contracts and rules of your environment. That said, ideally, governance is as hyperlocal as possible.

This enables people at similar stages in life to cluster and enjoy proper representation in their local jurisdictions. It also allows each person to move to more fitting locations as they evolve.

Overall, everyone benefits when all levels of awareness are honored and respected. A fair and just society must support the five levels of awareness by giving its citizens as much sovereignty as possible to follow their own life paths and live by their own truths. It must not get overly involved in people's lives. Instead, it must let things play out at the local level. The fewer overarching dictatorial forces, the more an individual's life can unfold on its own divine accord.

Of course, a society that supports all perspectives requires leadership that is aware enough to know that no single truth fits all. Unfortunately, throughout history, it has been extremely rare for such individuals to make it into positions of power. This is largely because highly aware individuals rarely feel called to play the power game, which is typically too toxic and not conducive to maintaining a balanced inner life. Still, occasionally, there is a highly aware prince, emperor, politician, or CEO.

It should be noted that the Five Levels of Awareness are evenly distributed across all functions and economic classes of society. The same majority of early-stagers are found in lawyers, teachers, engineers, lawmakers, and other highly credentialed positions as with the more menial, working-class population. So, it's completely unrelated to education level. There might even be an inverse relationship. It's hard to deny the impression that those who have spent the most time in the education system are also the ones who mostly live in their heads.

Being able to fulfill educational requirements and get a degree or certification is one thing. But emotional intelligence and spiritual awareness are completely different things. One is of the mind, the other about the essence of your being. The primary purpose of most modern education systems is to stimulate and develop the mind and emphasize knowing and planning. This is why a lot of self-work involves unlearning the limiting beliefs you were imprinted with during your academic years.

Interestingly, the same distribution of awareness levels also applies to nurses, doctors, therapists, and others in the healing professions. One would think that greater awareness prompts someone to choose a line of work where they can be of service. However, many things can motivate a person, including social status, money, family pressure, and any unhealed trauma. Therefore, having a degree or calling yourself a healer doesn't mean much without considering the person's level of awareness.

That doesn't mean that early-stagers are automatically bad at their jobs. It just means they're doing their best according to their abilities. It is up to you to decide whom to trust and give your money to. Most likely, you will choose someone who matches your sensibilities and frequency.

Even monks, clergy, religious leaders, and spiritual teachers are at different levels of awareness. Some see the scriptures' deeper meaning and intention, while others understand them more literally. As such, religious texts appeal to everyone in different ways at different times in their lives.

Looking at the great masters in any field, you can see how everyone's life experience has shaped their perspective and message to the world. Again, that doesn't make anyone superior or inferior. It just means their message will resonate with their particular audience. And if what the teacher has to say resonates with no one, then no one shows up. And that's all there is to it. An aware person knows that you don't need to be afraid of information that is different from what you believe in.

But the world is full of early-stagers who are deathly afraid of anything that usurps their sense of control and power. They insist on their beliefs being the sole truth that everyone else should follow. You see it in all areas of life, from alarmist activism, to hot-button social issues, to warring nations, to global elites who promise to save the world from itself. At Level 1, there is a preponderance of self-righteousness, narcissism, self-aggrandizement, and a thirst for control and power. Everyone thinks they're right, and the others are wrong. And it's all because they live in their heads, believing your thoughts, acting out their internal disarray. Their external behavior is just a reflection of that.

Whenever you see true injustice in the world, it's committed by people at lower levels of awareness. The simplest situations blow up and turn into a much bigger deal. Think family dynamics, where members lock horns and hold grudges for decades. Think office politics, where a misinterpreted email can set off a storm. Think national governments, where petty historical or ethnic differences are propagandized to drum up wars in which millions perish. Anywhere you look in the world, if something is messy, it's caused by people who live in their heads. Intelligence or being a good orator has nothing to do with it. Your level of awareness determines the place from which you act.

When viewed from higher levels of awareness, the world is chaotic and upside-down. However, when seen from lower levels of awareness, it is exactly as it needs to be to reflect and support people at earlier stages of their evolution. Living in chaos is one of the most important lessons that generate contrast and growth. You can't take that away from anyone.

As such, life on earth is not supposed to be at peace, nor will it ever be. Levels 1-3 occupy you for most of your reincarnation cycle. Levels 4-5 only take up the last bit of it before you graduate from Earth School and never come back. That's why you see so few upper-lever travelers around compared to the constant influx of early-stagers.

But while you're still here, the objective is simple: focus on yourself. That's the only thing you have a say over, anyway. Create the life you admire in others. Become the leader you look up to. Become the partner you want to attract. Speak your truth in the way you want others to speak theirs. Find the peace within you for others to enjoy and emulate.

LEVEL 5 | Paradoxes

There are very few paradoxes at Level 5 because understanding paradoxes is a big part of what gets you here. Those that remain speak to overarching themes that have accompanied you from the beginning of your journey and now have reached their peak.

PARADOX #1

To be enlightened is to accept that you're not.

If you want access to Level 5 oneness, you cannot think you're anything, including being enlightened. The moment you think you're enlightened, you're not. Thinking that you are, introduces a level of identification with being something, which immediately gives rise to a sense of self, pulling you out of oneness. Staying at the frequency of oneness means staying detached from anything you can conceptualize.

You can also see how *acceptance* continues to play a central role. It never goes away. The only difference is that you no longer have to make an effort at this stage—it's part of the essence of your being. Your complete embodiment of it is a pre-requisite for all Level 5 lessons.

PARADOX #2

You get there by wanting to be here.

Understanding and implementing this simple paradox can save you lifetimes of stuckness.

Continuing in the vein of *acceptance,* accepting where you are is what moves you forward. Induced highs from practices like shamanism, plant medicine, psychedelics, or letting loose at Burning Man—no matter how deep the insights they may bring—take you in the opposite direction, spiritually speaking, because the core motivation is you want to be someone you're currently not. There is a deep rejection of self in that. Not only do you not advance, you get even more lost. Your journey is about acceptance, acceptance, acceptance. Now, now, now. That's what brings you healing and moves you forward without ever denying who you currently are.

Unfortunately, your control-obsessed mind doesn't understand this. It thinks accepting your flaws makes them permanent. Therein lies the mental resistance and reactivity you must overcome. Of course, if that were easy, you'd start loving yourself right now.

PARADOX #3

**When you're comfortable being alone,
you're no longer alone.**

Once again, as long as there is resistance in you, you stay small. Resistance equals restriction. Your attention is consumed by whatever you're pushing back against and everything it brings up in you.

In this case, the fear of loneliness might tell you that you're not good enough, that you don't feel accepted, acknowledged, or seen, or that nobody cares about your existence. As long as any of those fears are still alive in you, being alone makes you feel lonely and unwanted. And – true to your fears – it keeps you cut off from the rest of the world.

Everything changes when you work through those fears. Now, when you're alone, you feel connected to everything there is. There are no longer any emotional barriers, energy blockages, or physical distractions keeping you small and separate. Instead, it's a direct line between yourself and the world. And - in the absence of limiting beliefs - you feel yourself expand to be as big as the world.

PARADOX #4

Life is a journey, but it's not.

You've heard it so many times: *Life is a journey, so don't get hung up on anything too much. Everything comes and goes.* This mindset has helped you get there, but it, too, is a crutch. There are only consecutive moments, which we must learn to be one with. There is no journey in oneness, no passage of time, no beginnings and endings. Everything just is, including you.

What got you to Level 5 is acceptance of each instance of form appearing and then fading. And so your whole life has been just that. Instances of form, arising and passing. Your relationship with each instance is what defines what arises next. Your entire purpose here has been to stop controlling the arising and passing and instead *be* the arising and passing.

LEVEL 5 | Summary

Level 5 is unique in that you must let go of everything that got you here. Nothing is added, only taken away. Through Meta-Awareness, you transcend your body, surrender to stillness, and just let yourself be, inviting the love that is everything to come forth and envelope you. At that moment, when all these elements come together, something fascinating happens. Everything collapses back into Pure Presence - but with one crucial difference.

At Level 5, you can no longer be aware of what's happening because you *are* the happening. You're not just part of it. You experience yourself *as* it. Harboring even the slightest hint of witness state would mean a sense of separateness, instantly taking you out of unity with your environment.

Instead, there is no environment in unity. You are purely present with everything *as* everything. You see yourself in trees and rocks, recycle bins, and street signs. There is no *other* in other people. There is no here nor there. There is no darkness, only light. Nothing has an opposite. Oneness is the end of duality and the continuation of infinity.

In Level 5 oneness, *you* don't exist. That means you are no longer aware of being aware. Rather, you are aware without knowing it. You *are* awareness.

At this point, you can see how it all stacks up. Becoming aware of your thoughts (Level 1) leads to letting go of control (Level 2). Letting go of control leads to accepting things as they are (Level 3). Accepting things as they are leads to continuous flow (Level 4). Continuous flow leads to oneness (Level 5).

You can see there is no right or wrong. There's no such thing as a mistake. You make decisions you feel called to make because there are still lessons to be learned at that place of life. And learning your lessons makes you more aware and moves you forward. There's no sense in resisting this system. This is how life works.

In summary, your journey takes you from being unaware of being unaware (Level 1), to slightly aware of being unaware (Level 2), to fully aware of being unaware (Level 3), to aware of being aware (Level 4), to unaware of being aware (Level 5). It's ironic that by no longer being aware, you become *one*. Or rather, you stop becoming. You just are.

The whole thing is quite brilliant because unity consciousness results from removing code rather than adding to it. It's like rolling back to a previous version of yourself – remember the completely unaware Level 1 state? The big difference is you've completed your journey. That grueling and treacherous journey, with all those twists and turns, is over. You've returned home – but with a clean engine. No more blockages remain. You're now part of the state where nothing exists. No baggage, no expectations, no limiting beliefs. And when nothing exists, everything is possible. And with that, the unaware state is suddenly the completely aware state.

A certain limit remains in that your human body is finite. It doesn't have energy forever. But by Level 5, the thread by which you connect to your physical being is incredibly thin. Do your best to honor your health and well-being, but there's no longer a need to cling to your physical life. You are literally on the verge of dissolving into another dimension.

Until then, you get to be the unfolding. The dancer and the dance. The light and the darkness. The real and the unreal. You get to be everything and the absence of it. When you only see where you are, there is nowhere left to go. When everything is simultaneously true and false, there is nothing left to doubt. When everything is equally valid and invalid, there is nothing left to judge. When everything you need is derived from being, you feel complete. And when you feel complete, there is no longer a *me*. You cannot be one with the world as long as you have a sense of *me* or *mine*.

As you can tell, Level 5 lessons are extremely subtle yet final and all-powerful. In more ways than one, experiencing yourself *as* the Universe requires leaving your body and earthly attachments behind.

To master Level 5, you must consistently inhabit Objective Reality. This naturally leads to your awareness expanding to include itself, i.e., Meta-Awareness. When you combine that with *being*, it creates an energy field free of resistance, and you become aware of the underlying stillness, the canvas of all creation. This awareness opens you up to merging with the all-pervasive, universal love.

Keep in mind that once you master Level 5, it isn't just the last level. It's your last lifetime. Save for some unknowable cosmic exceptions, you're not coming back after this. So stay focused to see this final stage through. Here are the main behaviors to check off and reflect on. You've mastered Level 5 when:

☐ You're aware of being aware all the time.

☐ You're completely surrendered to the unknown.

- You no longer need a separate meditation practice. You are in a continuous, meditative state.

- Your life is dedicated to being of service. You exist to contribute your frequency to the world.

- You no longer experience duality. Everything is equally important and unimportant.

- You no longer get lost in thought. There is no mind when there is no *self*.

- You never judge yourself or others. You let the world be.

- You're not afraid of leaving your body. A part of you is looking forward to it.

- It's extremely difficult to think about the past or future.

- You no longer experience time. Birthdays and holidays carry little meaning.

- Life feels like a game. Nothing is serious enough to get upset about.

- Life feels preordained. You're acting out your part.

- You live in profound peace, no matter what happens.

- You see the love of creation in everything.

LEVEL 5 | Next Steps

1. Practice Meta-Awareness. As you go through daily life, keep reminding yourself that *you're aware that you're aware.* The best time to do this is when you're in a low-intensity situation, such as standing in line at the supermarket, waiting for your phone to charge, or simply sitting on your sofa. Reflect on where you are or what you're doing, and notice that you're reflecting. Training your awareness muscle is like developing any other muscle. It gets easier and more natural with time. The most conscious state is when you're aware that you're aware all the time.

2. Practice surrendering. To explore the art of surrendering, expose yourself to topics or situations you've previously avoided, perhaps judging them as *too weird* or *esoteric*. The idea is to expand your capacity beyond the usual acceptance of things that show up, as things that show up are already part of the form dimension. Instead, you want to expand into the more formless realms of quantum physics, metaphysics, cosmology, myth, clairvoyance, the afterlife, and philosophy in general. This has the effect of opening yourself up to the unknown, which is essential to entering unity consciousness. Don't stress if you don't *believe* the things you read about. Just take in the information in a curious, non-judgmental way and leave it at that.

3. Be love. Practice seeing everyone and everything through the eyes of love. Don't just pretend. Don't just tolerate. Don't just accept. Be love. Your eyes are now God's eyes. Make an effort to see people you used to judge with unconditional, unadulterated love. You will notice that it's too difficult when your mind is involved since all thoughts are judgmental thoughts. Rather, see them from your awareness. Better yet, notice that you're seeing them from your awareness. And voila – you're practicing Meta-Awareness. It all flows nicely together.

4. Dissolve boundaries. That's right. All those healthy boundaries you've set – it's time to dissolve them. Getting to the point where you are so pure that boundaries are no longer needed is far healthier. All comfort zones require some level of judging, labeling, and separateness. It's fine. They have their purpose at lower levels. But now it's time to be completely fluid with everything. To live in unity consciousness, you can no longer put up any walls.

5. Get used to not wanting. Remember how Level 4 flow requires you to let go of your personal wants, entrusting yourself to what life wants for you? At Level 5, you no longer want what life wants for you because you no longer see yourself as separate from life. There is no longer a *you* that wants anything. As such, there is no need to distinguish between mind-made desires and divinely inspired ones because you're no longer in your mind. Deliberations and negotiations are non-existent because creation is instant and continuous. But *not wanting* cannot be forced. It's not an intention of the mind. It comes as a natural consequence of unity consciousness. So, if you find yourself not wanting anything, it means you're getting closer to the divine state of just being.

6. Maintain equanimity. Learn to stay completely in sync with the rising and passing of sensations in your body. Oneness requires a complete balance of the mind. From there, a broader receptivity emerges for seeing unexpected opportunities and insights that, in turn, lead to other unanticipated situations. This is how becoming an integral part of the co-creative process takes hold. You can test your level of equanimity by exposing yourself to multiple different environments over a short period of time. Even just visiting your family for the weekend is a good gauge.

7. See the aliveness in everything. Level 5 is about recognizing the inherent richness of life that your wanting and labeling has been blocking you from. This aliveness can be found in everything, from food to animate creatures to a rock. You can even sense it in the air, a pointer to the existence of that vast canvas of Stillness that underlies everything. To be connected to this aliveness is the most potent place you can be. It's the moment of life unfolding. All forms of thinking about it just get in the way.

TAKEAWAYS

Ultimately, The Five Levels of Awareness are pretty straightforward. You create situations that reflect who you currently are so you can get to know yourself better and make changes. The only question is, how aware are you when you make decisions? This informs the quality of the outcome and your experience along the way.

In other words, being more aware isn't about being more spiritual. It's about living the way life wants you to live by letting go of all the stuff that gets in the way. As your awareness grows, you don't stop living—you start living. You don't take less action—you take inspired action.

To recap, the following infographic provides an overview of the five levels and their core themes:

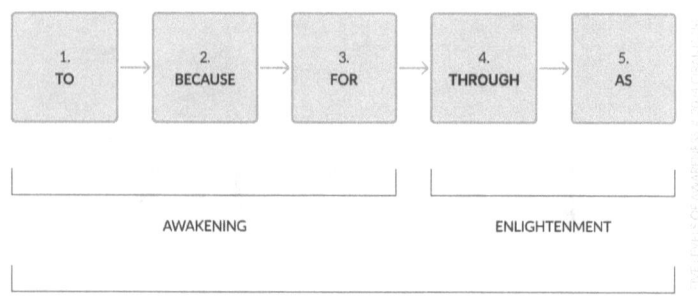

Level 1 awareness ("To") is where you spend most of your time defending what you already believe in, reinforcing and perpetuating your Subjective Reality. You cover up any sense of lack or not being good enough by pursuing outcomes you hope will fill the void. This is nothing to be ashamed of. Feeling motivated to have something because you dislike the feeling of not having it is one of the main building blocks of human behavior. You call them needs. Needs are what drive you to find solutions. At Level 1, however, you think that solutions are found in your environment. You think things are happening *to* you, and you improve your life by changing your environment. This is the changing-yourself-from-the-outside-in approach. Eventually, you realize it doesn't work. The fatigue from trying to fight life is wearing you down. And when it does, you're ready to try a different approach to life.

Level 2 awareness ("Because") is when you see the connection between your state of mind and how you experience the world. Little moments of self-reflection as to why things happen the way they do give way to growing insights that you are responsible for how you feel. You still seek refuge in avoidance behaviors and group activities, but the first cases of independent thought emerge. Eventually, you let go of control, and your evolution snowballs from there.

Level 3 awareness ("For") is when you start working on yourself earnestly. You become aware of your traumas and all the baggage and blind spots you've inherited. You also see how you've been manifesting situations from scarcity and lack of self-worth. This is when you reach the point where you realize you are no longer content with repeating old habits and running with the herd. And so, you focus on becoming a person with the qualities you admire in others. You may initially feel overwhelmed by all the stuck energy that comes to the surface and the limiting beliefs about yourself that have shaped your life. But you find a way to dig deep to work on yourself because you realize if you don't, no one else will.

Level 4 Awareness ("Through") is where everything you've worked for comes to fruition. You are led by the greater current. You are present with and inspired by the moment of creation. There is no delay in the happening and your experience of it. You are responding without resisting, manifesting without effort, deeply immersed in the simplicity of Objective Reality. If there ever has been a goal, Level 4 is it. But you're wise enough to know you get here by not wanting to get here. You get here by letting go of control and accepting yourself as you are, where you are. Only by holding everything as worthy, possible, and true are you a vibrational match to flow.

Level 5 Awareness ("As") is the state of no self. No self does not mean being selfless because selflessness is still only a concept that references a *self*. That means being selfless doesn't meet the Level 5 criteria of just being. Instead, Level 5 is about utilizing the power of love to become one with everything that enters your field of experience. You get there by surrendering every last shred of identity. By becoming nothing, you become everything. By becoming everything, you transcend duality.

AWAKENING VS ENLIGHTENMENT

Another important element of the graphic above is the delineation between awakening and enlightenment. These two terms are often used loosely and interchangeably. Therefore, it can be helpful to see them visually aligned with the five levels of awareness.

The first three stages encompass what is known as *awakening*. You gradually come out of blind ignorance to become more aware of the design of life. You go from *it's me against the world*, to *I play a role in the way things happen*, to *everything that happens is for my highest good*. During the awakening phase, parts of you might level up sooner, while other parts remain at lower levels. However, to graduate from the awakening stage, your life must be fully graduated across all aspects of Levels 1-3.

The last two stages represent *enlightenment*. This is where you drop all resistance and go with the flow, not just casually, but in the most profound, total surrender kind of way. You then cap off your earthly run by returning to your spirit nature and merging with the greater whole.

To unpack things even further, there are two kinds of awakening: spontaneous and gradual. The vast majority of humans are *graduals*. For them, awakening is a long, drawn-out process consisting of smaller breakthroughs over countless lifetimes. Even once a gradual recognizes that their primary purpose is to know themselves, progress is still slow, tedious, and incremental. The reason is simply that the brain is hardwired and takes time to be reprogrammed.

Spontaneous awakenings are rare. It's when someone experiences a sudden acceleration from a lower level – perhaps Level 1 or 2 - to Level 4. This usually happens in response to a survival situation. The individual has driven themselves to the brink of their existence through deeply unaware behavior and is completely and continuously lost in thought. Darkness and depression become so overwhelming that they reach a point where they either self-destruct or something inside lets go of control. As such, most spontaneous awakenings come from hitting rock bottom. Afterward, you still need a fair amount of time—at least a few years—to adjust to the new frequency. After all, the old Subjective Reality is physically embedded in your nervous system. Again, recalibrating takes time. However, the overall process is substantially accelerated.

Another, even smaller subset of spontaneous awakening doesn't happen out of desperation but rather out of glut. These individuals have achieved most of what the material world offers. They've accomplished everything society says will bring them happiness. Yet, something is still missing. That something, of course, is the connection to their inner world.

Whether you experience a gradual awakening or a more accelerated one, neither way is fun. Those who awaken spontaneously may have trouble re-organizing and re-integrating their life. Those who awaken gradually wish it would go faster. You don't really have a say in how it goes for you. All you can do is keep accepting where you are. What will be, will be.

PATH OF LEAST RESISTANCE

Lastly, you can see by the graphic above how each level builds on the previous. Everything has its purpose and place. There's no sense in complaining and wanting it to be different. If you want the smoothest, more direct path through your physical life, stop fighting your circumstances and start working with them. The single most powerful standout skill that moves you through the stages the quickest - while integrating lessons and honoring the overall design of life - is *acceptance*. From your first breath to the last, if there's one thing that should be at the forefront of every life experience, it's accepting who you are every step of the way.

INVERSE AWARENESS SPHERES

Another way to visualize The Five Levels of Awareness is by delineating how you experience them as you progress through the stages. But here's the crucial—and initially surprising—piece to understand: What makes the awareness spheres *inverse* is that greater awareness doesn't emanate from within. Rather, greater awareness means you're letting in more *Source*. The farther Source can reach inside you, the closer it gets to your core, and the more distinctly you feel its resonance and guidance. Source contains your creativity, wisdom, and physical vitality. It is your life force.

In fact, there's a natural pressure from the outside to compel you to let it in, as indicated by the inward-facing arrows. These are the lessons you encounter on your journey. As such, your evolution is not to control and expand to become someone new. It is to surrender and let go of who you're not. Life is intricately designed to make you more aware. With that in mind, examine the following infographic and then read the details below.

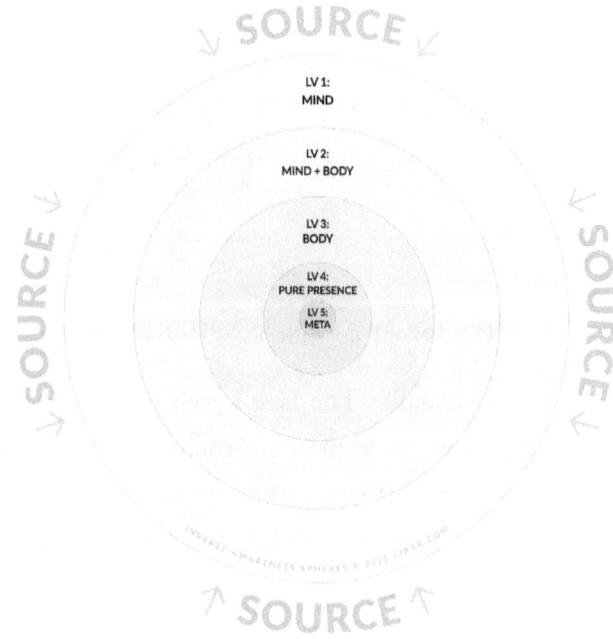

Level 1 awareness is experienced purely in the mind. At this early stage of your evolution, you are completely cut off from your intuition and exclusively use your mental capacities to navigate life. Again, lower levels of awareness do not equate with lower intelligence or socio-economic status. You could be a doctor, lawyer, professor, or CEO and be entirely driven by your identification with thoughts. Your truth is what you can rationalize.

Level 2 awareness is experienced through a combination of mind and body intelligence. This is when you get occasional intuitive hits in addition to the usual mental negotiations. At this stage, intuition is still something you ridicule and marginalize – largely as a holdover from Level 1 – so you're unlikely to consider it seriously. But you have the first glimpses into a world beyond your rational mind and physical senses.

Level 3 awareness is experienced by sinking into your body and letting what resonates guide you. It becomes completely normal to make even, or especially, the biggest decisions based on what feels right. At this point, you've tried living in your head enough to know it's not a happy place. Instead, you've realized how easy life is when you let your sensations lead the way and how unnecessarily hard you made in on yourself before.

Level 4 awareness is the state of Pure Presence. Here, you spend no time lost in thought. Rather, you are in the flow of the greater current, manifesting like a monster. In fact, you can't keep up with all the creative downloads. You have so few limits that you are a favorite recipient of the love for creation. You live at the spout of co-creation, which is described further down.

Level 5 Meta Awareness is beyond your regular awareness, hence the word *meta*. You're still connected to your body but in the faintest way. Instead, you freely travel through the ether as an infinite energy constellation, enjoying a seat at the altar of unity consciousness. You enjoy this frequency at the tail end of your human experience, and the only thing keeping you is fulfilling your purpose of being of service.

Unity Consciousness is when all spheres collapse, and the only thing remaining is unconditional, universal love.

THREE STATES OF CREATIVITY

Unless you're enjoying total Level 5 enlightenment – in which you are creation pure - you're likely struggling with staying in Level 4 flow because thoughts from Level 3 and below keep taking you out of it. The following infographic breaks down the Three States of Creativity and their associated characteristics. Take a look and then read on for more details.

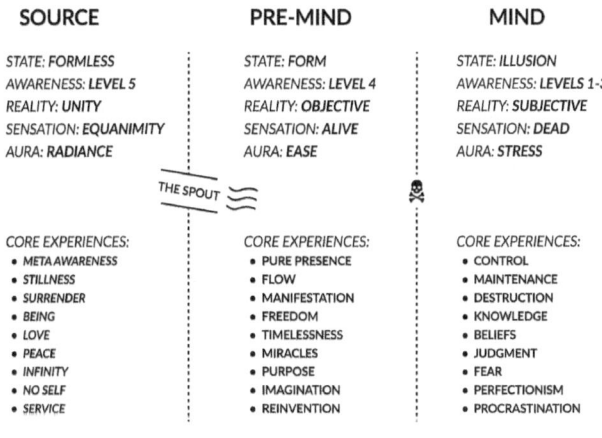

The Three States of Creativity are Source, Pre-Mind, and Mind.

The Source state is when you are one with the powers of creation. There is no thinking going on since your sense of *self* has dissolved. Almost no one is in this state, and if you were, you probably wouldn't be reading this book. It's much more likely that you find yourself at Level 4 and below. Hence, the focus is on how you receive information from the Source state.

As Source energy passes through The Spout, it enters the Pre-Mind state. The Pre-Mind state is Level 4. This is where you give shape to Source energy without being limited by low-frequency motives like fear, control, or judgment. You're at the height of your manifestation powers.

However, if your level of awareness is lower, Source energy doesn't stay in Pre-Mind very long. It quickly slips into lower levels dominated by Mind. This is where Source energy becomes severely impeded and often even entirely suffocated. Hence, the poison icon in the infographic above. It may sound harsh to say that the mind poisons Source, but it's pretty accurate. Mind is where you get stuck in boredom, procrastination, fear, and thoughts of *what if.* You might even say the Mind state is not a creative state at all. If you ever feel blocked or unable to focus, you know you're in your head.

To be the most creative and powerful manfester you can be, you must cultivate all the qualities that keep you in the Pre-Mind state, the state that receives Source inspiration, but before the labels and definitions of the Mind state kick in.

THE UNITY MATRIX

One of the most difficult states to describe is unity consciousness. You quickly discover how terribly inadequate words are. At best, language can only point to it. However, visualization is another realm of intelligence. As the saying goes, *a picture is worth a thousand words.* The following infographic captures the five elements of oneness and how to align them to enter that state.

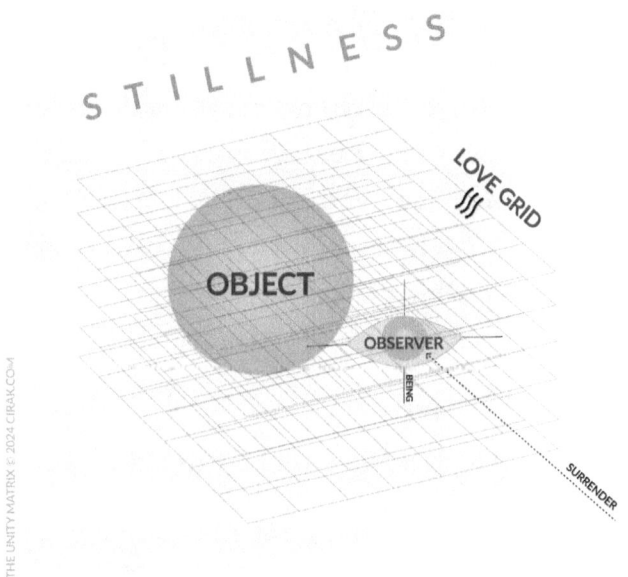

First, everything exists on the backdrop of *stillness*. Everything in the material dimension arises from and fades back into this stillness.

Then, there is a grid of love energy that permeates everything. In oneness, you can feel this love current flowing through everything around you, including yourself. This love energy is a thick, pungent frequency that has an equalizing effect on everything that exists. In the current of love, a rock is as significant as anything else. Everything on the grid is imbued equally with love by virtue of its sheer existence. Hence, the Object and the Observer find themselves as one, even if distinct at the level of form.

To enter the realm of stillness, the Observer needs to be in a state of *surrender*. Once there, *being* maintains its stable position on the Love Grid. Before any of this can take place, you need to detach from your physical self through Meta-Awareness. As long as your awareness is still tied to your body, you are not porous enough to join the Object on the Love Grid. You can also view it from off-grid and from separateness, i.e. Objective Reality.

THE FORM-SPIRIT LIFE HELIX

If you want to see your life progression both at the macro and micro levels, this next infographic does just that. Think of life as an infinite helix, an ebb and a flow of life that arises and passes. Each segment of this helix is an individual's journey. Examine the helix with one segment broken out:

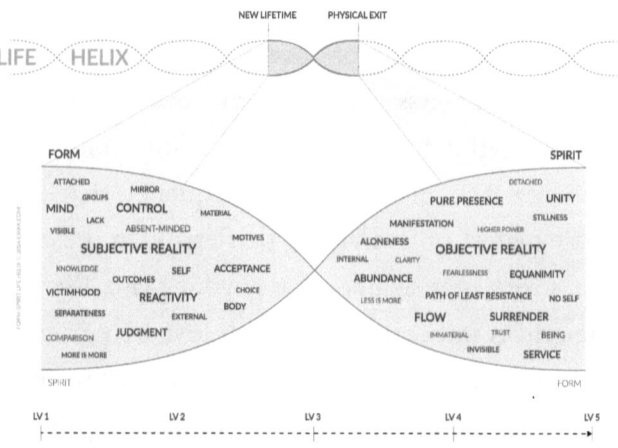

Each new lifetime enters the helix when Form is at its highest and Spirit is at its lowest. Over the course of your lifetime, your experience flips in that Form fades in importance, and Spirit gains in prominence.

Obviously, you are not guaranteed to make it through all levels of awareness with each incarnation. You might very well stay stuck at Level 1 the whole way through. But all levels are available to you at all times.

Also, there's no reason to be upset if you're stuck by the time of your physical exit. The next helix cycle is waiting and ready as soon as you regroup and get your priorities set for the next go-around.

The Life Helix also doesn't apply just to the material dimension. Your evolution continues in other dimensions. Only the tag clouds inside the helix change. But the rhythm of your life continues. For practical purposes, the above helis is shown on its side. But it should be pointing up to reflect your overall increased frequency.

Everyone is subject to The Form-Spirit Life Helix. For some, it may not be so obvious within a single lifetime that they're evolving. But over the ages, it becomes obvious. Even if you know someone who shows no interest in this subject matter, this could be a *rest lifetime* for them. Or one where they actively campaign against awareness. Remember, you need to experience contrast from all angles to diffuse the charge of limiting beliefs, learn to accept and let go, and move forward. So it doesn't matter if someone is going about their life in a way completely different than yours. They're in a phase where learning to live *that* way is the task. And *that* way is as valuable as *this* way. Thus, judgment is a complete waste of your time and energy. You're actually impeding their growth by pushing against them, even if only silently in your head. And not only is your resistance to who they are also holding them back, it's also keeping you small. Judgment is a lose-lose proposition. The sooner you let others be and focus on yourself, the sooner you become free to live your life.

NO JUDGMENT

It is imperative to reiterate that the five levels contain no judgment. They are never about good or bad, right or wrong, better or worse. They are simply about becoming more aware, dissolving blockages, and making decisions more aligned with your truth. They are never about blaming yourself for something you did when you were less aware. You learned from the situation, and now you're more aware. That's the whole point.

Why blame yourself for a situation from which you learned? Why feel bad about a decision that led to personal growth? Even if you have to repeat it a million times, each time is slightly different. Each time, you get a little wiser. Remember, you are the student, and life is the teacher. You're not meant to be enlightened instantly. You're not meant to be perfect off the bat. If you were, you would have no reason to exist. Recognize that it's all part of your learning curve. Everything in your life is always going according to plan.

IT'S NON-LINEAR

It's also helpful to understand that there is no clear delineation or discernible cutoff point as you move from one level to the next. There are many different interconnected parts to your evolution, and your awareness is never equal across all areas of life. You might be enjoying Level 4 flow in some areas of your life while still struggling with Level 1 blindness in others. Sometimes, it feels like you're leaping forward. Other times, you're regressing. Other times, still, you're stagnant. Just do your best to roll with it. Take one step forward when you can and two steps back when you must. That's why most of your journey feels so topsy-turvy. Again, this is by design. The disorder compels you to create order. It's the tension that drives you to seek calm. It's the chaos that motivates you to seek peace.

Awakening isn't a moment. It's a movement. It's the dawning that your life is a journey, that your work is never done, and that there is an intelligence at work far greater than anything you can know with your mind. It's the realization there is never a need for labeling, blaming, or judgment. Everything is always in motion. Nothing is ever something. As long as you keep flowing, you keep evolving. Problems only form when you stay inactive for too long.

THE ROLE OF MEDITATION

There is a common misconception in spiritual circles that being an astute meditator leads to enlightenment, and being enlightened makes you an astute meditator. Both assumptions are inaccurate.

Meditation should be seen and experienced as any other wellness activity that improves one's current state of mind. If one makes enlightenment a goal, one chases yet another outcome, limiting one's perspective and keeping one stuck.

As such, don't meditate to become enlightened. Meditate to engage with life in the most meaningful, efficient, and productive way. Here are three essential benefits meditation provides:

The first benefit of meditation is that it calms your mind. Less mind chatter, decreased reactivity, and an improved ability to stay present with what is in front of you result in immediate gains in concentration, engagement, and mental-emotional balance. You spend less time ruminating about the past and projecting into the future and more time enjoying the freedom of moving through the world on your own accord. Should you become enlightened one day – great! But again, don't do it for the future. Do it because you want a better life now.

The next benefit of meditation is that it promotes physical well-being in several tangible and measurable ways. It helps reduce stress and anxiety, lowers blood pressure, improves sleep, and relieves pain. It strengthens your immune system and can even reduce age-related memory loss. If not for spiritual reasons, meditation should be part of your daily routine for health reasons. Ultimately, you can define meditation as the practice of living a healthy, balanced life.

The third benefit of meditation is that it brings your intuition to the forefront. Meditation takes you out of your head and into your body, where your wisdom resides. Simply by being more aware of how you feel, you make better decisions and stay connected to your passions. Choice overload and analysis paralysis become a thing of the past. Constantly getting lost in thought fades. A dedicated meditation practice helps you avoid major pitfalls, dodge detours, learn your lessons sooner, and illuminate the path of least resistance. When you follow your inner voice, you navigate everyday situations from a place of alignment, flow, and inner truth.

PARITY

Objective Reality doesn't distinguish between a more aware person and a less aware one. It happens the exact same way, regardless of your level of awareness. There is complete parity. It's only your subjective interpretation that makes your life different.

At the enlightened levels, there is no friction between what is happening and how you perceive it. You live in fluid acceptance of how each moment presents itself. You still experience the ups and downs of life, but because you're coming from the grand perspective of flow and unity, your emotions are diminutive, uncomplicated, and navigable. You still have days when there's more flow and days when there is less. You still have days when their meditation is blissful and days when it's not. You still experience the joy of success and the grief of loss. In short, an enlightened person is not above anything. They're not better or more deserving in any way. Rather, they are fully engaged with life without interfering with it. They don't spend time on things that don't matter, which – at lower levels of awareness – is most of what you believe and do.

If you feel bogged down by your current life situation and think that what you read here only applies to those in more fortunate circumstances, take these words to heart: The difference between an inspired and fulfilled life and a lethargic and dissatisfied one is not your circumstances. It's what you do with them.

Everyone gets hurt. Everyone has trauma. If not their own, they inherit it from their lineage. The patterns of how we get hurt – emotional neglect, not feeling seen, feeling judged – are basically the same, regardless of your economic or social circumstances.

In fact, just being born can be traumatic. Just getting acquainted with the physical dimension can cause one to develop perceived issues and shortcomings. There is no such thing as the perfect parent. Most families and societies operate at Level 1. Everyone gets traumatized during their upbringing, often by the most innocuous circumstances.

Perhaps as a toddler, you went shopping with your mom, and right when you needed a hug, she turned to get something from the next aisle. And boom – you spend the rest of your life dealing with fear of abandonment. Or your dad didn't show up to your soccer game because of a work deadline, and now you feel unloved. Or some kid makes fun of you at school, but instead of firing back to defend yourself, you keep quiet and bury your feelings of shame deep inside.

You can see how these scenarios transfer into various settings later on. You didn't get a hug when you needed one to establish a healthy sense of trust, so now you take that insecurity into your adult relationships. You might start a family because you want to feel the love you didn't get as a child. Or you struggle to ask your boss for a raise because you didn't learn to speak up in your formative years. These issues can impact you for decades and limit your entire life's fortunes.

Have you ever wondered why certain life situations have impacted you deeply while others who experienced similar walk away unaffected? Why did growing up in the same household influence you one way and your siblings another way? Why do some people march forward, undeterred by rain and storm, and make it to the mountaintop, while others are discouraged and remain at the foot of their hill?

It's too simplistic to blame your life circumstances for how you feel. You can't undo the past. What you *can* do is look within and dissolve any lack or limiting beliefs before you manifest big situations from them. That way, you don't bring your trust issues into your relationships. Or you learn to love yourself before making your kids responsible for it. Or you work on releasing stuck energy in your throat so you're ready to speak up at the appropriate moments.

Everybody is somewhere on the path. No one is not on their journey. The process is relentless, but you cannot fail. At times, it's agonizingly difficult. Other times, it's pure bliss. Learn from the blows and enjoy the highs. One day, they will be a distant cosmic memory.

Enlightened people may come across as divinely gifted to those mired in the chaos of their minds. But they're not. Everyone can learn to quiet their mind. Peace and balance are your natural state. The greatest teachers of all time all resoundingly send the same message: Do not follow, do not admire. Instead, be like them. Recognize the qualities they represent, and find those qualities within yourself. They're there. All you have to do is look.

PERFECTIONISM

Perfectionism deserves special mention because most people are conditioned to believe that making a mistake is the worst thing you can do. Growing up, you've felt the judgment of others and have internalized it as there being something wrong with your personality. This gives rise to a fierce inner critic. Ironically, everyone thinks everyone else is thinking about them, which means nobody is thinking about you.

Self-judgment is extremely harmful and limiting. Your inner critic is always looking for ways to make you feel like you're not good enough, not deserving enough, or not capable enough. Most of your negative self-talk comes from thinking you should be perfect.

Even positive judgments carry a harsh nature. To say *you are this or that* is a character attack, regardless of how well-intentioned.

But you're not supposed to be perfect. You're not supposed to be Superman or Wonder Woman. You're not supposed to know your life ahead of living it. You're supposed to be a learner. That is nothing to be ashamed of. Rather, learning is the most exciting, rewarding state. Learning keeps you open, curious, inviting, and in awe and wonder of yourself and the world. Discovering your passions, skills, and what you're truly capable of is the greatest adventure. Failure means you're taking action. You're moving forward. You're exploring, trying things out, seeing what resonates and what doesn't. You're building momentum. What others think doesn't matter. You're not doing it for them. This is your life. You're doing it for you.

Ultimately, there is no such thing as an unaware person. It's simply a question of degrees of awareness. Everyone is always aware - in all the ways they need to be - in order to grow. Even Level 1 awareness is still awareness. In fact, even the least-aware person is still incredibly aware. They might have anger issues, but they still love their children. They might struggle with addiction, but they still honor their parents. They might live in chaos, but deep down, they wish they could bring order to it. They might struggle with their actions, but their heart is in the right place. They might do everything right but want to live more from their heart. Sooner or later, everyone's behavior will match their inherent desire to be whole. You cannot blame anyone for anything. Everyone is doing their best.

That includes you. You're always making decisions to the best of your abilities. Should you realize in hindsight that you should do things differently – perfect! Do that next time. This is the learning process. Life is designed to move you from barely aware to completely aware. Lack of awareness drives your awakening. You learn your lessons, wise up, and make better decisions. In the end, you graduate from Earth School. There is no issue other than believing you should already know everything from the start.

The core trait of enlightenment is knowing you can't know anything. You can't know if something is good or bad. You can't insist on your plan because life will show you otherwise. The secret to a meaningful life is letting it unfold and getting to know yourself along the way. All peace and purpose come from letting things be. So stop pretending you need to know everything. Stop pretending you can predict the future. Stop letting your fears control you. You're a learner, not a loser. You're a container, not a complainer. You're a winner, not a whiner. You grow when you flow. You excel when you let go.

You think you're supposed to know it all. But you're not supposed to know anything. Knowing takes you out of the flow. It disconnects you from Source. Knowledge is an illusion, anyway. It's based on a snapshot of a moment under certain conditions that is in the past. How reliable is that? Is that the best foundation from which to make decisions? Thinking you know shuts you down. It kills the magic. The moment you know something, it's dead.

REGRESSION

If you've experienced regression therapy, you might wonder how awareness affects reincarnation cycles. The answer is simple: Every new life starts out with Level 1 awareness, even if this is your *nth* lifetime.

The difference is those with more lifetimes under their belt move through the remaining life lessons quicker and, thus, up the awareness ladder sooner. That said, re-entry into the physical dimension is such a shock that even the most enlightened soul needs a moment to find their bearings.

Being unaware of past lifetimes has a purpose, of course. It ensures fresh perspectives and new approaches in this lifetime. It acts as a kind of amnesia, preventing you from falling into worn grooves from before. You're much more likely to try new things, go down new roads, and seek new adventures, which fosters broader personal growth and spiritual evolution. Otherwise, following the same old patterns would lead to stagnation.

Some of your past still trickles through in the form of inexplicable talents, unfounded phobias, languages you speak but never learned, or deja-vus. But for the most part, you forget about past lifetimes quickly and focus on the current one. You become infatuated anew with being incarnate, which leads to forming new attachments and suffering, eventually motivating you to break out of the things that stifle your growth. It feels a bit cruel by design, but this is not the time to question universal reasoning. The reality is that you would never leave your comfort zone if you didn't get challenged. Your body, your mind, your being... everything requires a certain amount of stress to stay healthy and keep expanding. Life is designed to provide you with enough stress, even when you learn to come out of reactivity.

For those of you who believe this is your only lifetime, reflect on how much anxiety, urgency, and disorientation this creates in you. But don't worry. You transcend it as you move through the stages and recognize yourself as infinite. On the scale of infinity, even those who have no interest in spirituality learn and grow. But if you have an interest – as evidenced by reading this book - you can consciously accelerate your journey and minimize the suffering that would eventually push you to deepen, anyway.

SHORTCUTS

Human nature is to avoid pain, even when it's directly related to growth, which it always is. Hence, you might be inclined to look for shortcuts in your spiritual evolution. You might think you can skip the lessons of the awakening stage and jump straight to enlightenment.

Every day, somewhere in the world, people take mind-altering drugs in a variety of settings in an ongoing attempt to break the stranglehold of their conditioned minds. This is nothing new. Since ancient times, organic and inorganic psychedelics and various forms of sensory deprivation and amplification have been used to induce heightened states of awareness and extract negative energies. Participants marvel at ecstatic insights far beyond their usual scope. And while that's the goal, that's also the problem.

How you respond to everyday situations physically manifests across your entire personality in your reactions, judgments, and programmed behaviors. It is physically manifested in your nervous system. So, while your brain may catch incredible glimpses of your uninhibited self, your holistic being includes many more mental, emotional, physical, and spiritual components – and those don't change from one moment to the next.

Hence, once you come down from your high, you have no practical way to hold those insights in your being in a meaningful and permanent way. Your capacity to hold higher frequencies simply hasn't developed yet.

Furthermore, the environment you return to is still the same environment that both reflects and reinforces your old ways. In most cases, the energy of your insights fades, and all you can think of is planning the next escape so you can catch another glimpse.

On the surface, it looks like you're trying to break free from who you are and become a better person. But you've learned by now that results are dictated by your motives. In this case, your motivation to partake comes from resistance, desperation, denial, and rejection of your current self. Energetically, instead of expanding, you're cementing who you don't want to be.

You only do drugs when you don't like yourself. Or when you've lost trust that life has your best interest at heart. Or when you're avoiding old wounds. Or when you feel lonely, lost, and depressed. Or when you want to numb the pain of being you, or rather, how you think of yourself.

Of course, one could argue that even drug-induced experiences are part of that learning curve. Many who use psychedelics eventually come around to realizing everything they need to awaken is already within them. But is this the energy you want to grow your life from? Do you really want to awaken out of lack, ego, fear, or self-loathing? You might gain some insights, but you risk developing miscues from the forced fracturing of your energy field. At best, you could spend entire lifetimes karmically deranged, tediously working through very nuanced circumstances to try and iron it all out. At worst, it's possible to permanently damage the spiritual guardrails on which your life rests. You can become energetically unhinged when you force yourself to confront truths before it's your time to see them.

Why risk all that when life has already designed a perfect process for your highest good to ensure your fullest evolution? All you have to do is accept things as they are right now. And then the next moment, and the next. Acceptance is the quiet, clean, and direct path of least resistance. Taking drugs is a loud, dirty path full of resistance and detours.

If this is you, don't fret. And don't blame yourself. You're in the perfect spot to make changes. Your desire is noble. You want to stop suffering. You want to feel like you're enough. You want to love and be loved. You want to be free of anxiety and fear. You want peace of mind and a positive outlook. You want to feel like your life has meaning. You don't want to look in the mirror and see a problem that needs fixing.

The good news is you're more aware than ever before that most of your suffering is self-generated, and if you learn not to judge your feelings, they become very manageable. You know that lack is an unhealthy place to manifest from. You know, the less you try to repair yourself, the less you feel broken. You know that real power doesn't come from rejecting yourself. It comes from acceptance, stillness, being, and love. Just like you have the capacity to see yourself as a problem, you have an even greater capacity to be the solution.

That said, all change is gradual, and for good reason. Changing how your entire system processes information is highly intricate, with many interdependencies reaching deep into your psyche, body, and energy field. Comfort zones are meant to keep you safe and contained. You wouldn't want your nervous system to be able to shift suddenly, which would bring a troubling degree of volatility and instability. Change must be incremental so your whole being has time to adjust to a completely different way of interacting with the world—one that is energy-flow-based, not mental-control-dependent.

Therefore, change should only be undertaken gradually, organically, and in full synergy with the whole self. And that's what day-to-day life does for you. That's why each level of awareness takes so long. Sudden or extreme jolts don't stick and, worse, can scramble your brain. If some parts are cracked open before the whole self is ready, synapses become jarred, confused, and fire out of sync with one another. This can result in a divide between the part of the nervous system that has seen the true nature of reality and the one that is still anchored in the old. Instead of feeling better, it can lead to feeling more triggered and agitated than ever, creating even more inner conflict. You may see through the fallacy of the life you've lived so far but not know how to accept it. You may be aware of all your imperfections but unable to make peace with them. You may see how you get in your own way but are unable to cultivate flow. And throughout it all, the energy of self-rejection remains unaddressed.

It's frustrating to the mind, but this is what happens when you don't like yourself and think you can fix it by escaping into extreme, altered states. This reflects the core issue of living from and for the mind. It looks for solutions outside of itself because - out of self-preservation - it cannot admit that it itself is the problem. Over decades, it has built a fortress of mental truths. It has defenses like you wouldn't believe. Just doing some breathwork or focusing on a candle will have the mind throwing fits to maintain control. Only once you start meditating in earnest do you realize how it won't give you a millimeter without a monumental battle.

People have and will continue to do drugs and try to attain enlightenment because living life the *normal* way is so hard. It's so hard to surrender your beliefs. It's so hard to embrace the impermanent nature of life. It's so hard to let go of control. The tipping point is when you realize it's much harder to stay in control. Much harder to maintain an artificial truth structure. Much harder to cling to moments and try to make the past last forever.

Inherently, drug use is neither wrong nor right by itself. Nothing is. It's simply a question of objectively considering possible consequences. That means factoring in the hazards of inexperienced practitioners, tainted substances, or the chance of seizures, psychotic breaks, and physical ailments. It might include the time and effort of prolonged aftercare, mood swings, depression, and wrestling with an overall inclination for escapism. It might involve damage to friendships, relationships, careers, and finances. It might mean seeing things you can no longer unsee but that your mental-emotional-material constitution is not yet ready to support. Do what you must do. Just be aware of what you're doing when it's motivated by not liking yourself.

If you're interested in scientific research, studies on the brains of monks show how meditation can generate the same chemicals that fill the receptors that get you high when you do drugs. And that's the difference: External injection of chemicals is temporary. Self-cultivated chemicals are permanent because your entire endocrine system has evolved over time. You can't escape yourself. You can only accept it.

COMMITMENT

Looking at the five levels and everything it entails, you might wonder how big this commitment is to living a conscious life. The answer is pretty simple. You live in a universe of cause and effect. Where you put your attention is where you experience the most growth. Spending more time at the gym builds physical muscles while meditating cultivates your awareness muscles. Going to a theme park with your kids nurtures the family bond while enjoying a sound bath soothes your inner garden. When you spend your time chasing outcomes and herding stuff into your attic, you eventually find yourself confronting feelings of emptiness and disillusionment. When you take time each day to sit in stillness, you nurture peace. It's up to you where to put your attention.

The best part is that you don't need to wait for judgment day to reap your rewards. When you live and act in alignment with your truth, you are instantly rewarded with good feelings. If you go against it, you are instantly punished with bad feelings. Your life is a direct relationship with energy, and meditation sensitizes you to this energy.

For those who think meditation alone is the answer, think again. Your environment is designed to be a powerful mirror for a reason. You can't work on yourself without it. Even monks must engage with each other, the monastery, staff, guest meditators, etc. And when they meditate, they still have to deal with their thoughts. You get to know yourself better by living life. Not by escaping it. Life is the ultimate revolving door of learning and growing. Your job is to stop pushing against it and accept that it never stops turning.

The commitment to yourself doesn't have an end date. There is no finish line. Focus on cultivating inward stillness, outward vitality, deep embodiment, and mental clarity. What other state would you want to be in?

You did not dream of yourself. What makes you think you're less than the dreamer? You were not derived from lack. What makes you think you're less than infinity? You did not create yourself. What makes you think you're in control of your life?

Not being in control is not a detriment, anyway. Quite the contrary, you could not accept a greater gift if you tried. Unbeknownst to your earlier selves, you are being offered the chance to partner with the forces of creation. To be an incubator of the unknown. To transcend yourself and become one with all there is. To be loved and to be love. To experience yourself more perfect than you ever imagined.

To be aware is to dance with God. You're given all the time you need to practice. Just remember what an honor it is to be on the same stage.

"FROM"

And so she sets out to live her final life with abandon, driven by divine intuition, feeling the ever-relentless beat of her heart, to give of herself one last time and complete her mission. She is ready to be seen from hiding so long. Ready to be heard from being met with silence. Undeterred from feeling lost. Unrestrained from overcoming conditions. Fearless from living with fear. Ignited from struggling to find light. Nurtured from feeling unheld. Softness prevailing from falling hard. Lightness pervading from lifting herself up. Unique from losing herself in the crowd. Confident from feeling unworthy. Accepting from being rejected. Open from being shut down. Surrendered from holding on to dear life. Standing strong from giving up. Wise from knowing so very little. Caring from being careless. Loving from a broken heart. Whole from feeling incomplete. Grateful from losing everything. Healed from hurting so bad. Her highest self from deepening so much. Awakened from sleeping in the dark.

EXAMPLES

Different levels of awareness result in vastly different approaches and responses to all areas of life, including lifestyle, education, medicine, law, freedom of expression, and partnership. Here are some of the most common ones to help you get a sense of where you currently stand.

RELATIONSHIPS

Level 1: I don't want to be alone.
Level 2: I want someone who makes me happy.
Level 3: Let's help each other heal and grow.
Level 4: I want a relationship where I can be myself.
Level 5: I like you, let's see where this goes.

MARRIAGE

Level 1: Getting married will bring me love and status.
Level 2: I want someone to procreate, grow old with.
Level 3: Being married is the ultimate mirror.
Level 4: I'm ready to reveal every part of me.
Level 5: I'm ready to be of service through sacred union.

CHILDREN

Level 1: Having children will give me love and purpose.
Level 2: I want to be a better parent than mine were to me.
Level 3: I work on my issues so I don't put them on my kids.
Level 4: I feel called to procreate, even though it's hard.
Level 5: I am divinely guided.

DIVORCE

Level 1: My life is ruined. They will pay for this.
Level 2: I'm not an angel but it's mostly their fault.
Level 3: It takes two to tango. Let's split amicably.
Level 4: I support us growing in different directions.
Level 5: I honor you for being part of my journey.

HEALTH

Level 1: I have [condition]
Level 2: I am dealing with [condition]
Level 3: My body is experiencing [condition]
Level 4: My body is sending me a message.
Level 5: I am always getting stronger.

MEDICINE

Level 1: Give me a quick fix pill.
Level 2: I should get another opinion.
Level 3: Show me the alternatives.
Level 4: I know myself best.
Level 5: True healing starts from within.

HAPPINESS

Level 1: Life is unfair and makes me suffer.
Level 2: If I achieve [outcome] I'll be happy.
Level 3: I'm responsible for my happiness.
Level 4: There is no reason not to be happy.
Level 5: Happy is my natural state.

SELF-LOVE

Level 1: Self-love is selfish.
Level 2: If I buy nice things I'll like myself more.
Level 3: I'm working on accepting myself fully.
Level 4: Me-time is my favorite time.
Level 5: When you love yourself, you love life.

ABUNDANCE

Level 1: Everyone else has more than me.
Level 2: I must work hard to get my piece of the pie.
Level 3: I'm getting better at receiving.
Level 4: I can manifest unlimited abundance.
Level 5: I am enough.

FAILURE

Level 1: I'm afraid of failure.
Level 2: Others fail too sometimes.
Level 3: Failing means I'm moving forward.
Level 4: I'm always learning and growing.
Level 5: When one door closes, another one opens.

SUCCESS

Level 1: You can't always have what you want.
Level 2: If I achieve [goal] I will be seen as a success.
Level 3: I do things for me, no matter what others think.
Level 4: Being true to me is all that matters.
Level 5: I am here to serve.

CONFIDENCE

Level 1: I am not good enough.
Level 2: If I achieve [goal] it will make me confident.
Level 3: I'm working on letting go of limiting beliefs.
Level 4: Life always works out.
Level 5: Everything is possible.

EDUCATION

Level 1: I must get good grades to make my parents happy.
Level 2: Good grades lead to a safe job, house, retirement.
Level 3: There's more to life than grades.
Level 4: I enjoy learning about things I'm interested in.
Level 5: I am the student. Life is my teacher.

TRUTH

Level 1: I'm always right and you are wrong.
Level 2: I'm always right, but I tolerate your opinion.
Level 3: You are entitled to your truth.
Level 4: I support whatever you believe.
Level 5: Everything is true.

FORGIVENESS

Level 1: Those who did wrong don't deserve to be forgiven.
Level 2: I can forgive, but only with certain conditions.
Level 3: I forgive to let go of the negativity within me.
Level 4: I don't hold grudges to begin with.
Level 5: Everyone is always doing their best.

GRIEF

Level 1: I'm going to feel like this forever.
Level 2: It's going to take a long time to feel better.
Level 3: I'm actively working through the pain.
Level 4: I accept my feelings as they are.
Level 5: I let difficult feelings strengthen me.

ANXIETY

Level 1: I'm debilitated by this feeling.
Level 2: It's going to take a long time to feel better.
Level 3: I'm learning to observe my sensations.
Level 4: I can feel anxious and still move forward.
Level 5: I am everything I feel.

FUTURE

Level 1: I'm deeply afraid of the unknown.
Level 2: The more I plan, the less I'll be afraid.
Level 3: I am learning to accept where I am.
Level 4: I look forward to see what happens next.
Level 5: There is only now.

DEATH

Level 1: I avoid thinking about it at all costs.
Level 2: It's an unfortunate part of life.
Level 3: I'm learning to accept it.
Level 4: My time will come when it comes.
Level 5: Ready when you are!

www.ingramcontent.com/pod-product-compliance
Lightning Source LLC
Chambersburg PA
CBHW060552080526
44585CB00013B/530